Bringing Learning Home

Bringing
Learning
Home

*How Parents Can Play a More Active
and Effective Role
in Their Children's Education*

Mary Susan Miller

1817

HARPER & ROW, PUBLISHERS, New York
Cambridge, Hagerstown, Philadelphia, San Francisco
London, Mexico City, São Paulo, Sydney

FIRST EDITION

Designed by Ginger Legato

U.S. Library of Congress Cataloging in Publication Data

Miller, Mary Susan.
  Bringing learning home.

  Includes index.
  1. Home and school. 2. Parent and child.
3. Children—Management. I. Title.
LC225.M53 1980   649'.68   80–7856
ISBN 0–690–01952–1

81 82 83 84 85 10 9 8 7 6 5 4 3 2 1

To

Mammy and Doc

... for loving

Contents

Acknowledgments

I am indebted to

Amy Gittell for her critical eye, her honest voice, and her nimble fingers. They helped me write this book.

The people who have touched my life as students, and their parents and teachers. What they enabled me to experience is the substance of this book.

The questions and answers found at the end of chapters 1–9 have been excerpted from my "Between Parent and Teacher" column, which appears monthly in the *Ladies' Home Journal*. I have grouped them according to subject matter and placed them in the chapter of the book that deals with the area of their concern.

These are real letters from real people about real problems. They represent your problems. In answering them, I hope I am answering your questions as well as theirs.

If the day and the night are such that you greet them with joy, and life emits a fragrance like flowers and sweet-scented herbs, is more elastic, more starry, more immortal—that is your success.

Henry David Thoreau

Introduction

Some years ago, representing the National Association of Independent Schools, I served on a committee of the nation's leading educational organizations. The group had been formed to address itself to the problem of communication between colleges and nongraded schools—that is, schools that do not give marks.

Around an enormous conference table in the offices of the National Association of Secondary School Principals sat about twenty men and women from associations covering the field of education from elementary school to college. These people had experience. They had knowledge. They had clout.

As we set about our work, hope ran high within me—hope that I feared had been snuffed out during many years of frustration as a teacher and a principal. So much was wrong with education; like the weather, it was something everyone talked about, but no one did anything about.

At last, here was a group that would do something. How excited I was to be part of a team that was going to solve the problems in education. We were going to find The Answer.

The committee met for a year and a half at regular intervals. Traditional and alternative schools were the focus. We discussed the relative rate of acceptance of students from each kind of school—but we never questioned the relative value of their programs. We related the accuracy of predictions of student success to high school grades—but we never looked into what was happening to the students as people. We compared teacher preference in evaluating students with letter grades and percentages—but we never wondered how the students felt about themselves.

When the committee decided that its work was completed, we had nothing more to show for our efforts than a standardized form for alternative grades, intended to clarify communications between nontraditional schools and colleges.

"Now that we've settled that," I dared to say, "let's get down to education."

A few people laughed, uncomfortably.

"No, I mean it," I went on. "Let's use our combined know-how and decide what the goal is that we are looking for. It certainly can't be just grading systems."

It turned out, however, that it *was* grading systems because the committee went no further. It disbanded—this group of educational leaders—with a form for alternative grades to leave to education's posterity.

We never found The Answer.

Because we never asked The Question.

And that seems to be the story of education.

Actually, The Question is an easy one to ask. It should be basic to every school and every school system. It is simply this: *What should educators be trying to do?*

The Answer, though, is difficult. It means defining the goal of education. And when educators seek to do that, they have to broaden their vision; they have to define the goal of life. Because that's what education really is—getting ready for life. Schools give students tools to build a life with. But if educators fail to have their own conception of life's goal, or at least do not incorporate that goal into their teaching, how can they help the students use those tools effectively? Amazingly, schools today often teach students reading and math but neglect to emphasize *why* and *when* to use these skills.

It would be like giving someone a hammer, a needle, and a checkbook—and not saying whether the task was to build a house, sew a dress, or balance a bank account.

I have seldom heard educators ask themselves, or each other, what they want to accomplish in the long run. They keep haggling over the day-to-day problems of teachers and grades and basics.

They are willing to discuss for a professional lifetime the relative merits of phonics and sight-reading, but they don't seem to ask, "What can we do to help children stay excited about reading?"

They argue endlessly over the value of grades as a way to motivate students, but they don't ask, "How can we learn to harness a child's own inner drive?"

They study curriculum to keep up to date with trends, but they give little attention to finding a way not to kill a child's natural curiosity.

They devise medals and honor rolls as systems of reward, but they rarely wonder about how they can help kids find their own satisfactions.

They figure out ways to offer remedial help to failures, but it doesn't seem to occur to them to ask who the failure really is—the child or the school.

Educators are so busy determining the tools with which they want to equip their students that they have little time left to draw a blueprint of the life they hope their students will create. If they come to realize that the fulfilled life—not day-to-day academic achievements—is the goal of education they will then be forced to ask the question, "What makes for a fulfilled life?" In answering, educators will have to look into the lives of the people they turn out—and into their own.

What is fulfilling? Success, of course. But what is success? Attaining affluence, prestige, possessions? We used to label people who achieved such things "successful." But we are learning that material values do not bring true success. No, rather, success is what people bring to themselves, not what they gather from the outside. Curiosity in the mind, creativity in the imagination, energy in the body, self-confidence in the spirit, love in the heart—these are the qualities that fulfill, that bring success, that shape the good life.

Are schools helping to teach these qualities? Few that I have seen.

If such qualities shape a life well-lived, should they not then be the goal of education? Yet no committees appear to promote this goal. No schools build it into their curriculums. No teachers are trained to write lesson plans incorporating it. No report cards inform parents as to how close their children come to reaching it.

Above all, most educators are not even considering this goal. They discuss methods and course content and grading systems instead, coming up with different answers every decade or so. Progressive education doesn't work now, so we try traditional. Before we know it, traditional isn't working any more, so we go back to progressive.

We know something is wrong, but we don't look far enough to determine what it is. We just keep coming up with changes, specific ones concerning *how* we teach and *what* we teach. As a result, schools fail to improve.

Actually, the how and what of teaching are insignificant without the why. How can teachers teach effectively when they have never thought about the purpose of their teaching past the final examination or graduation? What difference does traditional or progressive education make if the teaching is not directed at enriching a student's life?

Instead, we give children the idea that learning is about achievement. They always seem to have to be getting somewhere in school: from first to second grade, from junior high to high school, and so on. They are pressured to go from a C to a B in English, to get into the Advanced Placement class, to make the varsity football team. When they are out of school, they still think they have to be getting somewhere—from one job to a better job, from a small house to a bigger house, from a cheap car to a more expensive one. How can they ever be fulfilled? They must continually achieve to prove their worth. They can never rest.

The truth is that learning is not *getting* somewhere but *being* somewhere. It is responding to the moment with the full relish of your five senses, not pushing past it to reach another moment that lies ahead. Reading, for instance, should not be evaluated by how quickly you can read a stack of books but by how lusciously you devour one. That's why Robert Frost taught a course at Amherst College called "How to Be a Slow Reader." Similarly, living should not be measured by the speed of upward mobility but by the intensity of the joy of lingering where you are. That pause is what learning—and life—are all about.

When educators do concern themselves with helping children reach that goal, their committee reports will be more meaningful than an alternative grading form. They probably will not try, however—unless parents insist.

Unfortunately, parents were once students too, in achievement-oriented schools. They are the kids caught in the "success" syndrome—all grown up. Some have realized that what they struggled for in school may not have been worth the effort of twelve years. All the pressure and strain and worry about achieving during those school years did not add to their adult life; in fact, what *was* worthwhile, what they might have been learning at the time, passed them by. It isn't their fault, though; they only did what they were told and taught.

Other parents are still pushing hard, as they did in school, and are trying to "get there." They haven't yet learned that "there" is nonexistent. So they perpetuate the illusion by joining forces with educators to help their children relive their own experiences in school—even though they may have been unhappy there and may still be unhappy.

This book is an attempt to break the lockstep.

I am a parent, and I want to tell parents that they can make a difference in their child's education. They *are* the difference.

I am a teacher, and I want to tell teachers that there is another way.

To both, I want to say that a better education does not take more money—it takes more effort in thinking and planning about where schools should be heading.

Both parents and teachers are unhappy with schools as they exist in most parts of the country today, yet neither sees a way out. They feel that children are being deprived of a chance to learn, yet they do not know where to turn.

I say, turn to each other. Form a partnership. Then, together, turn to your children. It is to them that education is ultimately directed. Try to discover what they need; then demand that your schools provide it. Your children are probably closer to defining the real goals of education than you are—especially the young ones who still believe that discovering is more fun than being told, that experimenting is more fun than being right.

This book is an attempt to get parents (and teachers) to look at school as a community made up of students, teachers, administrators, *and parents,* all working together. I will explore with you the many facets of a child's education, in the hope that a new viewpoint will present new possibilities.

"I never looked at it that way. Let's give it a try."

That is what I hope you as readers of this book will say to yourselves. I can't expect to change the basic system of education through this book, nor can I expect administrators and teachers to unlearn all they have learned in college, and through their own experience, and reeducate themselves. All I can hope for is a new awareness that lets you begin to see the possibilities for alternatives and changes in your schools. I want you to realize that there is no need to sit passively by as your children are being educated in ways with which you do not agree. A parent can, with hard work, help make a child's education a positive, creative experience. All you need to do is start with the question, What should the school be doing for my child? The answer lies not in what is *found* but in what is *sought.* Seeking the goal of education is what learning is about. From there, the world of change is open.

Twenty years ago, like most parents and teachers, I didn't think in terms of educational goals any further than the final exam. I taught narrowly, refusing to veer from my course outline. I taught rigidly, restricting my students' interests to my own. At home, I saw my children not for the individuals they were but as the stereotypes I had been brought up to expect.

A product of traditional parents, I had no more awareness of the many dimensions of growth than they did. But I learned, as I saw my children cope far less well with emotional situations than with academic ones, that the prescribed ways of educating children—both at home and at school—cut off areas of human development essential to a full life. Loving my own children opened my eyes to the uniqueness of *all* children. Caring for my students helped me seek ways to meet the needs of *all* students.

At last, my children and my students became real learners. At last, at home and at school, I became a real teacher.

With enough concern and effort and thought, we can all become teachers—*and learners.*

1/Motivating Your Child

The air is tense. Silence hangs in the room so heavily that a dropped eraser echoes. Heads bend stiffly over desks. Hands cramp around ball-point pens. The junior class at Louver High is an hour into the English final.

Marsha raises her hand for another blue book, not lifting her head. She turns the last pages and keeps writing. Every night for a week she has crammed. Having nearly failed the midterm and pulled down a C for the semester, she had enraged her parents.

"This is a warning, young lady. Next time you'll be grounded for a month," said her father.

"If you can't go out with your friends, you'll be forced to study. You have to pull up those marks," said her mother.

"I will. I'll do better. I'll study hard for the next exam."

Next semester is now as Marsha writes feverishly.

Allan leans back, stretching his neck until his face parallels the ceiling. Rolling his shoulders, he hears a bone crack. The proctor hears, too, and smiles.

"Allan's our student," his mother always announces at family gatherings. He can hear her voice as it poured across the table at Easter dinner last month. "Top of his class two years in a row."

It means a lot to her. Next year she can say "three years in a row." Allan returns the proctor's smile and leans back into his work.

Janet hates English. No matter what her teacher says, she

still thinks Jane Austen is boring. Gerunds, participles, noun clauses—why does she need them? She is going to marry Greg and have three children. She wants that ten-speed bike, though.

"Have you done your homework yet, Janet?" That has been Dad's routine question every night since the third grade. She would hear it for the rest of her life, revolving like an endless record in her brain. She always did her homework. Dad made it worthwhile—a dollar for every A in grammar school, two dollars in junior high.

Now a bicycle—a blue beauty in Webster's window. Janet looks at her watch. She sighs, blows her nose, and starts writing again.

Mr. Harwood teaches Marsha, Allan, and Janet. They are his favorite students. They work hard. They appear to be motivated. Mr. Harwood wonders how motivated, though, when the first question they ask when they get back papers and exams is "What did you get?"

They *are* all motivated students. But motivated by what? Marsha is motivated by fear of punishment; Allan, by need for approval; Janet, by a dangled reward.

The school reinforces their motivation by stressing marks. They read the Honor Roll; they post rank in class. They run a highly competitive business.

"What's wrong with competition?" Janet's father asks. "It makes the kids work."

He does not think to ask whether it makes them learn.

"What's wrong with competition?" many parents ask. "We live in a competitive world. Better to train the kids for it."

They do not think to take a closer look.

Yes, we do live in a competitive world. We compete to get a job, to make the most sales, to bake the best cake in the Pillsbury contest. We compete on the Saturday tennis court, as husband–wife teams in bridge, or alone in golf or at the bowling alley. We may compete to be the best dressed in the crowd or to give the wildest parties, to tell the funniest jokes, keep most abreast of the news, or hold the highest-paying job. We win some, we lose some. The competitive game is a life-style. It stimulates. It challenges us to do our best. It teaches us to win gracefully and lose amicably. Good stuff, competition. Good to keep you on your toes.

THE GROUND RULES OF COMPETITION

Competition *can* be constructive. It was not, however, for Marsha, Allan, and Janet. It can be positive when the competitive field is entered under three conditions:

Condition No. 1. The competitor makes the choice whether or not to enter the race. She decides to put her cake alongside the others. He decides to be the neighborhood fashion plate. They decide to tee off or serve or roll the ball. No one forces them to enter the game. They elect to play.

Condition No. 2. The competitor knows the ground rules. Hoyle has seen to it, along with every association from Lawn Tennis to Tiddledywinks, that games are played by the rules. Players are aware of them at the outset. They cannot circumvent them. The rules do not change midway. Competitors enter the game on sure footing, knowing what to do and how to do it and knowing their goal: to knock down the most pins, to bring home the biggest paycheck, to have the most important acquaintances or biggest car or most intellectual conversation. They make their moves toward that goal.

Condition No. 3. The competitor feels confident. No adult is forced to enter a tennis tournament at the country club. Mary stays out of it if she is poorly coordinated. No adult is required to become a salesman. Peter chooses another career if he is shy. The poorly coordinated woman, however, may write beautiful poetry; she enters a magazine poetry contest. The shy man may be a whiz with figures; he becomes a top CPA. Adults select their competitive arena according to their talents. They enter knowing that they have a chance of winning. They may not win, but they *can*.

What about young people in school? Is their competitive field subject to the same three conditions? Is their competition constructive to growth, or is it defeating?

1. Do students choose whether or not to enter the

competition? No. The law demands that they be tested and marked and ranked. Their parents demand top performance. And the kids—they can demand nothing. They keep running the race under pressure. Those who drop out bring shame to themselves and their families. Those who rebel bring punishment. The majority, unwilling contestants, play the game.

2. Do students know the ground rules of the competition? No. The ground rules in any competitive game indicate a winner and a loser. Kids understand that. Here is something, however, they do not understand: Who is supposed to lose in education? Isn't everybody expected to learn? The ground rules are unclear. Even teachers find them confusing. Every student is supposed to learn; how do you manage to find losers in the competition?

Well, you can mark on a curve. That is one way to solve the problem. You are sure to have a required number of winners and losers. Or you can pass the kids along to a higher level of work even when they haven't learned the lower level. That is another way to solve the problem. You will create dependable losers year after year. Or maybe you can label kids with marks— "He's a D student . . . She's a B student." People (even the students themselves) will believe the labels, and they will perform up—and down—to these labels.

No, the ground rules of education are not clear to students.

3. Do students feel confident in the competition? No. A boy is a slow reader, but he still has to compete in English. He is not as lucky as the shy man who can choose a career other than sales. A girl is weak in math, but she can't walk out of the math exam that she is taking alongside the math genius. She is not so lucky as the poorly coordinated woman who chooses poetry over tennis matches.

Every day of their lives, young people in school face competitive situations in which they feel inadequate. Picture yourself having to play tennis against Björn Borg. The stakes are high—your reputation, your self-image, your future. You are scared, resentful, ill-equipped, embarrassed. That is how millions of young people feel in school every day.

The foundation of learning is the feeling of "I can!" With

the feeling of "I can't!" the child backs away, fearful even to try. You can say, "Forget it," and walk off the court if Borg appears. But schoolchildren have to stay in the contest, often facing what they believe to be failure.

The three conditions under which adults enter competition, therefore, are denied to their children. As a result, what is for adults an exhilarating experience, a challenge, becomes a tool of destruction to their children. Having no choice of entry, they feel helpless. Unsure of the rules of the game, they grow confused. Inadequate to meet the competition at times, they lose self-confidence. They are constantly pressured to perform, to conform, to be better and best. Yet only a few scattered schools dare to break the competitive lockstep and reach out for other motivating forces.

Let me point out quickly, as parents usually do in their defense, that certain areas of competition are constructive for young people. Trying out for the school play can be a test of courage. Even if the part is not won, self-confidence may be. But no student is forced to audition. Each does it by choice— with hope, and perhaps even visions of stardom. Furthermore, every student is well aware that only a few get the coveted roles. That is constructive competition.

Entering a drawing in the art show, trying out for the basketball team, representing the fifth grade in a spelling bee: all these are competitive and all abide by the three conditions set forth: choosing to enter, knowing the rules, feeling adequate. Under these conditions, the contest can lead to growth—and to fun. Unfortunately, pushy parents can destroy even these kinds of competition by perverting them to a "win . . . or else" situation for their child.

The battle of English III leads even less to growth when the goal is the mark at year's end. It may lead to cheating or new ways of releasing pressure or dropping out of school—but not necessarily to a love of English.

Parents who motivate their children competitively are not helping them to learn. They are, instead, teaching their children that the satisfaction in studying and working hard comes from winning. And they are losing sight of the most important fact of all—that the learning process, not mere fact-getting, takes place only when the desire to learn comes from within. Children cannot learn in order to please someone else—but only when the joy and excitement of discovery are their own.

THE PARENTS' ROLE IN MOTIVATION

What can you do to help? Forget marks. Look beyond the A and the F on report cards. Look, rather, into your children. Forget pushing them to be "best." Help them learn. Help them grow. Help them to be happy in school

"How can we do that?" you ask. "How can we go against the school?" You are still the prime movers in the lives of your children. You can combat negative competitiveness by being aware of it. First you have to believe that there is a better way, and then you can take specific steps.

Deemphasizing Grades

No matter how loud the Honor Roll reading in assembly, no matter how shiny the gold stars in kindergarten, you can keep grades in perspective. You must abandon giving rewards for good grades and giving threats, scowls, or punishment for bad ones. That is relatively easy, but more difficult steps are to come; you must abandon parental status seeking as well. No longer can you boast to family and friends, "Our child got all A's." Look to your own competitive winnings for status.

When report cards come home, parent and child should review them together. A report card can be used constructively by parents to see where learning, growth, and improvement have or have not taken place. A mark of D raised from an F should provoke pride in some cases. If a B has dropped to a C, this should evoke questioning in others. Was there a problem? Has it been corrected? How can we help? Should we discuss it with the teacher? Marks are shorthand messages that parents can learn to read. They are not medals of honor, nor are they the shameful sign of Cain.

Straight A's, which please the hearts of American parents, may indicate far less learning than scattered failures do. The child who fails may be the one who has dared to try something new—as was the case with the schoolboy Albert Einstein. F's leave far more room for learning than A's do and give lessons broader than those memorized from the textbook. F's open the possibility of discovery, whether of subject matter or of self. The late John Berryman, poet and philosopher, understood the value of failure. In describing a mediocre figure in our midst, he said, "He could never succeed on a grand scale because he could never fail ignominiously."

Let parents ponder that at report-card time!

Motivating Through Cooperation

The family as a cooperative team offers the perfect hands-on learning experience for children. There it is, a living laboratory of motivation through cooperation—the exact opposite of the school's motivation through competition.

Dad and, in many instances, Mother bring home money that is used jointly. If the family adheres to American stereotypes, Dad lubricates the car, even though Mother and Junior use it. Mother cooks dinner, even though Dad and Junior eat it. And Junior, what does he do? He puts his blocks away so Dad won't stub his toe. He sets the table for dinner so Mother has time to read the evening paper. He gets his homework done on time so the family can go to the movies together. And he tries to avoid fights with his little sister for the sake of everyone's peace. They live on a tiny kibbutz—a self-contained venture—even amid an ocean of competition.

When parents nag children about schoolwork or keep pushing them to do more and do better, they break down these team interrelationships, tenuous at best under the normal family tensions of sibling rivalry, parental conflicts, and such. Enemy camps are set up—children against parents—a competitive situation that never (and I say, after 17 years of experience, *never*) makes children become learners. It makes them defensive and rebellious or apathetic and withdrawn, but it never gains the ends for which the parents are battling.

Instead, parents should help see home and school as part of the same cooperative effort. Junior goes to school, as Mother and Dad go to work, because that is what helps a family operate. If parents slack off on their jobs, other family members are made less comfortable; there is less money, less security. Similarly, if Junior slacks off in school, Dad acts angry, Mother nags, little sister teases, Junior builds defenses, and the family is again in turmoil.

The father of a sixteen-year-old boy took me to task about this cooperative approach. "That team stuff doesn't work with my kid. I tried it with his homework last night, and he still didn't do it."

Of course not! You can't wait until your child is sixteen. And one night won't do the trick. You have to begin in the first grade.

Some schools devote part of a year of social studies class, usually in the primary grades, to the investigation of communities. Children learn the various roles of the fire department, police, post office, etc., visiting each in turn. The children enjoy walking through the neighborhood in lines; the teachers count heads and sigh with relief when the 3:00 P.M. in-count tallies with the 9:00 A.M. out-count. Municipal workers create goodwill and have some laughs with the children.

Parents can continue this unit and take it as far as the school should take it. For the community, like the family, is a living example of cooperative motivation. When each department performs its job well, a community flourishes.

But, of course, many towns do not work. Like the family disrupted by divorce, the community gets disrupted too. Children can learn from this also if parents help them. Parents can take the isolated bits of news and conversation that children hear—about strikes, air pollution, inflation, crime, unemployment, etc.—and help children fit them into a larger picture. The non-functioning community can be just as good a lesson in cooperation as the functioning one. Where did it go wrong? What are the interdependencies, and which segments fulfill their responsibilities? What could be changed? Children who are made aware of these issues can mature by learning how to solve them.

Children learn best by *doing*. As family and community members, they are *doing*. Parents can use the opportunity to show them *what* they are doing and *how* they are doing it. As parents, you should learn these lessons yourselves and, in learning, teach. For teachers and learners too are interdependent. Children sensitized to their interrelationships with members of the team on which they play—the family, the community—learn a new and lasting motivation. They learn the strength of cooperation amid a competitive world.

Teaching Self-Motivation

I have pointed out that the real goal of education—if educators would stop inventing tests and rewriting curricula long enough to address themselves to it—is preparation for life. And who will be there to provide motivation when teachers and report cards have disappeared from view? Obviously, only the individual. How successful is the school that produces lifelong learners! Unfortunately, self-learning is overlooked by most schools. Teachers are supposed to have the answer. Students who seek in their own nooks and crannies and discover their own answers are often labeled uncooperative and receive F's.

A fourteen-year-old boy articulates the pointlessness of this system. "I was so busy studying that I didn't have time to learn," he says.

In the final analysis, we all teach ourselves. Others may lead or guide or coerce, but no one can really teach another. We learn. The thrill of discovering this secret, this power, is darkly kept in educational archives—or, perhaps, not even known there. Yet it can be one of the wonders of a child's life. And parents can reveal it.

Children teach themselves to walk, to talk. They teach themselves about eating and playing games and making friends—lessons far more complex than the simple ones in school. They can, then, just as easily teach themselves the lessons that teachers try to teach—and with less scolding, punishing, and scowling.

Reaching a Goal

Jimmy taught himself to tell time because his mother let him wait on the corner for his father every evening at 6:10. His mother could have announced, "It's six-ten, Jimmy. Time to meet your father." However, she was wise.

"You learn to read the clock," she said. "Then at six-ten you can go meet Daddy." Self-motivation was the lesson along with the clock-reading.

Mary wanted to pay for the groceries at the supermarket when she and her mother went shopping. Her mother could have counted out the bills and let Mary hand them to the clerk. But she too was wise.

"How can you pay at the store until you know how to make the right change?" Mary learned how to handle money.

When Kathy was in tenth grade, she began to talk about driving a car.

"There's no sense learning to drive if you don't know how a car works," her father told her. "Anything can go wrong. You'd better be able to fix it."

Kathy began a year-long self-taught course in auto mechanics. By the time she was old enough to get her driver's license, she was the class expert.

It is easy to help your children use their natural curiosity and desires as goals for self-motivation. You need only be imaginative enough to recognize the situation when it presents itself—and loving enough to give your children the privilege of struggling. Your child will do the rest.

Giving Pleasure

While self-motivation in the cases described came through desire to achieve a personal goal, it can also come through a desire to give someone pleasure. We have all seen the meticulous care with which a child makes a Mother's Day card or builds a wooden shelf for Father's birthday. The child enjoys the labor of love.

You can extend this joy into learning. Your child can be encouraged to read in order to read a story to the family; to practice the piano in order to play at Sister's birthday party; to work on penmanship in order to write a letter to faraway grandparents.

Let it be noted, however, that being motivated by the desire to please someone is quite different from motivation for approval. In the former case, the child works to make someone happy; the motivation contains the pleasure of altruism, something we all strive for. In the latter case, the child finds acceptance and self-worth by doing what someone else thinks should be done. The former is self-directed; the latter is other-directed.

Children come equipped with the motivation to work to make someone else happy. Can any parent forget a child's smile in extending a dirty hand clutching dandelions and grass? Or the fallen cake? Or the crayon drawing? Or the lopsided Valentine? "It's for you." Children want to work; all parents need to do is let them.

Finding Fulfillment

The ultimate goal of self-motivation is, of course, personal fulfillment. When Brian spends all morning building a garage out of blocks, he works for the satisfaction of it. Similarly, as he grows older, he selects a book from the library and reads it for pleasure. Both tasks are difficult, but he is motivated to pursue his efforts out of personal fulfillment, as we adults tend a garden or sew a dress or jog a mile.

Too often parents take the satisfaction out of those efforts with their nagging and scolding. They quell the child's natural curiosity and enthusiasm and simply take the fun out of learning. When parents relax enough over issues such as homework, children experiment and explore on their own. Self-motivation becomes compelling, and children learn what their parents were pressuring them to learn anyway—but at their own pace, in their own way.

The baby sitting on the floor tearing newspaper into irregular bits is far from the primary school child identifying triangles—and later the high schooler studying theorems in geometry; yet one evolves from the other. The baby laughing over the "Alphabet" record grows into the child uncovering the wonders of Dick and Jane and their equivalents—and later into the reader of *Frankenstein* or *Jane Eyre*.

The so-called open classroom, a derivative of John Dewey's "progressive" school, aims to make this transition smooth and easy. It guides children to motivate themselves for personal fulfillment. Unfortunately, many teachers are too inexperienced to handle this kind of teaching, and many parents are too anxious for their child's achievement to accept it. As a result, this type of learning through discovery has become the subject of considerable controversy. What a shame! It is a child's own natural way toward growth. Despite conservative retrenchment, however, many schools throughout the country have adopted open-classroom methods to support their philosophy of learning.

And you can adopt this kind of teaching-learning in your own home. All you need to do is follow your child, whose interests will lead to hundreds of learning experiences. Try following those interests rather than imposing your own.

At the beginning of this chapter we met three teenagers who worked hard because their parents directed them. None of them knew the joy of self-motivation. None of them had the fun that learning can be. Ironically, none of them achieved the goals their parents had thrust upon them. And their parents never understood why.

Competitiveness, as learned in school, has not produced a world with which most of us are satisfied. At the personal level, it leads to inner conflicts that can twist personalities and distort relationships. At the public level, it leads to fear and hostility and sometimes even war.

It is time to find alternatives. Children are the people with whom to begin, for they are malleable. Home is the place to begin, for that is where the kids are.

You need not be the helpless victim of a school system (or of a world system) in which you no longer believe. You are in control. You can help shape the world to come.

Dear Mrs. Miller:

How can I get my three teenagers to read this summer? It is enough of a struggle during the school year when they have to. What on earth can I do when they don't even have assigned reading?

Jane T.

Dear Jane T.:

Let me start by suggesting what you should not *do. Don't nag your kids to read—that is a sure way to turn them into television addicts! Books can be fun—even to your children—if you help them regard them that way. After all, they won't have to read textbooks this summer; and they won't have to write book reports or make oral reports; best of all, they won't have to be tested on what they read. The pressure is off. They can select whatever interests them from hundreds of thousands of books. That gives them independence; it puts decision-making in their hands. You know what weight that carries with teenagers. Start your kids off by giving each one an End-of-School present—a book dealing with a subject of special interest to him/her, be it automobiles, movies, fashion, or sports. Then see if your local library has youth programs over the summer—speakers, book clubs, parties, and other activities that would draw them. Here's an idea I have seen work: as a family, go to the library together. Let each member select a book (Mom and Dad, keep yours relatively easy) and read it. Then rotate the books until all of you have read all the books. Good dinner conversations should ensue. Above all, let them see you read . . . and don't be afraid to limit TV.*

Dear Mrs. Miller:

The school our eight-year-old goes to is terribly competitive. The teachers drive the kids for marks, and the children compete and compare all the time. We don't feel this way, and we don't like what it is doing to our daughter. How can we counteract it?

Mr. and Mrs. T.G.

Dear Mr. and Mrs. T.G.:

Congratulations! Just asking your question means you have the problem licked. Let your daughter know— repeatedly and in many ways—that school is for learning, not mark getting, and that learning is fun. Let her

*know too that learning often entails trying and failing
and trying again and discovering. That's why failure is a
positive experience, not a negative one to be stigmatized
as it is in school. Give her unpressured learning experiences at home and in the community so she will understand and believe what you are saying. However, make
her aware that school plays by other rules, so she will
know what to expect. As for you, stick to your guns; don't
fuss too much over report cards and gold stars and Hon-
or Rolls.*

Dear Mrs. Miller:

Our ninth-grade son, Jeremy, is not a very good student—
mainly because he isn't interested and doesn't apply himself.
We think he needs to be disciplined and sat down in Study
Hall forcefully. Instead he has volunteered to tutor a third-
grade child who is having trouble reading. It cuts out one of
his study periods every day. Do you think he should do it?
The school says "Yes."

Mrs. Joan F.

Dear Mrs. F.:

*I say "Yes" too. Student teaching has been found in
school after school not only to help the younger child but
to reinforce the older one as well. I have seen it turn on
the bored kid, activate the lethargic one, kindle warmth
in the unfeeling, and turn the misbehaving into a solid
citizen. Jeremy is undertaking a serious responsibility—
maybe for the first time in his life. He will feel depended
upon, and he will have to follow through. This alone will
build his self-image. When you add to it his satisfaction
in seeing the third-grader's reading improve, you will see
a young man ready to grow. The best student is not the
one who sits longest in Study Hall but the one who feels
good enough about himself to want to study. Three
cheers for Jeremy and his school . . . and to you when you
say "Yes."*

Dear Mrs. Miller:

We have two children, a seventh-grade girl and a tenth-grade boy. Nina gives us no trouble. But Dean is driving us crazy. He won't do his schoolwork no matter what we do—scold, plead, threaten, reason. Is there any way left?

Parents on the Brink

Dear P.o.t.B.

I suggest three ways that are left: 1. Stop pushing. Your son is grown-up enough to assume responsibility for his schoolwork. Urge him to discuss the situation with his teachers (you may have to go with him) so he will have the facts and face them realistically. Don't let him live in the dream that "Everything will work out." It won't, unless he works it out. 2. Try to find out why he doesn't do his schoolwork. Asking him outright will probably not bring forth the reason. Is his sister getting all the praise and affection? He may feel it is futile to compete with a paragon and may have given up. If that's not it, try to think of other underlying reasons. 3. If numbers 1 and 2 do not bring about a change, make an appointment with the school psychologist.

Dear Mrs. Miller:

My husband and I are both college graduates, and we feel that our children should have some intellectual interests. But no, all our daughter (sixteen) thinks about is boys, and all our son (fourteen) wants to do is play the drums. They couldn't care less about schoolwork. Why?

Jane and Joe W.

Dear Jane and Joe:

Your kids sound normal to me—after all, sex and rhythm are pretty basic, aren't they? At sixteen and fourteen, they are pretty absorbing too; it is difficult to have energy left over for math and grammar. Still, they shouldn't be completely turned off. Here are a few questions to ask yourselves: 1. Are you pushing too hard? Maybe the kids are rebelling. Relax. 2. Are you forcing them to fit into your image of success? Maybe they would rather not try at all than to fail at it. 3. Is the teaching at school traditionally dull? Try enlivening it by carrying it into your home and community—family projects, trips, etc. 4. Have you overindulged your children by doing things for them? If so, they expect you to keep doing it, to make learning easy. Stop. Let them learn to struggle . . . and grow.

Dear Mrs. Miller:

Janice, who is in tenth grade, simply will not read. She does her assignments, but she never picks up a book just for fun. My husband and I read a lot and can't understand her. What can we do?

A. and J. N.

Dear Mr. and Mrs. N.:

My first thought is, Have you pushed reading so far that Janice is rebelling? Think about it. If so, discuss the situation with her, admitting your overeagerness and at the same time pointing out what pleasure she is cutting herself off from. If it is not rebellion, could it be the lure of television? Here are a few suggestions to combat it: 1. Set up a family read-aloud hour every evening, letting Janice pick the books. 2. Let her stay up a half hour past her usual bedtime by reading in bed. 3. Talk to your local librarian and see if she has any interesting programs suitable for her age. If not, you might think about starting one. 4. See if she will volunteer to read to a younger brother or sister or to children in a home or hospital. 5. Make sure you aren't giving your own reading more attention than you give Janice.

2/Getting Along with the Teacher

These rules were posted for teachers in a New York school in 1872:

All teachers take note:
1. Teachers each day will fill lamps, clean chimneys.
2. Each teacher will bring a bucket of water and a scuttle of coal for the day's session.
3. Make your pens carefully. You may whittle nibs to the individual taste of the pupils.
4. Men teachers may take one evening each week for courting purposes, or two evenings a week if they go to church regularly.
5. After ten hours in school, teachers may spend the remaining time reading the Bible or other good books.
6. Women teachers who marry or engage in unseemly conduct will be dismissed.
7. Every teacher should lay aside from each pay a goodly sum of his earnings for his benefit during his declining years so that he will not become a burden on society.
8. Any teacher who smokes, uses liquor in any form, frequents pool or public halls or gets shaved in a barber shop, will give good reason to suspect his worth, intention, integrity and honesty.
9. The teacher who performs his labor faithfully and without fault for five years will be given an increase of twenty-five cents per week in his pay, providing the Board of Education approves.

By 1923, things had eased up a bit. The following contract was used in Idaho:

Miss————————agrees . . .

1. Not to get married. This contract becomes null and void immediately if the teacher marries.
2. Not to keep company with men.
3. To be home between the hours of 8 P.M. and 6 A.M. unless she is in attendance at a school function.
4. Not to loiter downtown in ice cream parlours.
5. Not to leave town at any time without the permission of the Chairman of the Board of Trustees.
6. Not to smoke cigarettes. This contract becomes null and void immediately if the teacher is found smoking.
7. Not to drink beer, wine or whiskey. This contract becomes null and void immediately if the teacher is found drinking.
8. Not to ride in a carriage or automobile with any man except her brothers or father.
9. Not to dress in bright colors.
10. Not to dye her hair.
11. To wear at least two petticoats.
12. Not to wear dresses more than two inches above the ankles.
13. To keep the schoolroom clean: to sweep the classroom floor at least once daily; to scrub the classroom floor once a week with hot water and soap; to clean the blackboards at least once daily; to start the fire at 7:00 A.M. so the room will be warm at 8:00 when the children arrive; to carry out the ashes at least once daily.
14. Not to use face powder, mascara or paint the lips.

Things have changed somewhat. Still, the teacher's lot is not a happy one in the 80's. Teachers are reproached by administrators for disorder, blamed by parents for low reading scores, scorned and sometimes even beaten by students for insisting on standards, and considered problems by the community whenever they complain. Worst of all, many teachers today cannot even find classrooms in which to subject themselves to the pains of their profession. Tenured teachers hang on, while new teachers are forced to become real estate agents and salespeople. Those graduates fortunate enough to land positions find that teachers' colleges do not always prepare a young teacher for the problems that occur in classrooms.

"They taught me how to open windows for the best ventilation," one young woman gasped after her first two weeks. "But they didn't talk all that much about kids." She faced a fifth-grade class of thirty-one children with reading levels from first to eighth grade.

"I learned four methods of teaching the novel," a new English teacher sighed. "All I do now is break up fights." He might as well have switched education courses with a woman who complained that all she learned in college was how to write on the blackboard while facing the class. Not bad for self-defense!

THE TEACHER'S JOB

Despite all we read and hear about teachers in schools, very little attention has been paid to defining their actual jobs. This is a major difficulty. What exactly are teachers supposed to do? Whose standards should they follow? Whatever they do, they are accused of doing it badly. What is their job? The answer depends on who is speaking.

Administrators want their teachers to make the school look good. They want kids kept *in* and drugs *out*—to keep the community off their back. They want basic skills taught well enough so that test scores will be acceptable—to keep parents off their back. They want teachers to be fair, fun, and friendly—to keep students off their back. Educating so many students, so diverse a population engulfed in such all-encompassing problems today, school administrators survive mainly by avoiding trouble. The ally who can help them most is the classroom teacher. What do they want? No trouble.

When students speak, they claim to want their teacher to teach. Of a group of students questioned recently as to why they are attending school, almost 90 percent answered, "So I can get a good job (or into a good college) when I get out." Young people today want their teachers to prepare them for the trade of earning a living. They want them to give them the skills of reading, writing, and arithmetic, along with other necessities. They want teachers to *give*—to make them learn. The world has not conspired to help them understand that learning is *taken*, not *given*.

When parents speak, they cry for success: they want the teacher to give their child an A. Too often they forget that education is a process of growth, not of achievement. A normal step in that process is failure. Jonas Salk experimented a hundred times before discovering polio vaccine. A child plays with a thousand letters before discovering "A." Education is not the victorious shout, "I have won!" It is the cry of wonder, "I see!" Still, parents demand success of their children's teachers—the gold star and the "A."

What of the teachers themselves? What do they say?

"Teaching is not a job. It is a way of life," says Myrra Lee, 1977 National Teacher of the Year.

"Teaching? It's living through the day," says another.

To one teacher it is "a commitment to life's most precious resource—children."

To another, it is "being a damned baby-sitter."

One fact emerges as practically universal, however. A teacher who enters the profession today does so with a desire to change the world and with hope. Let any unbelievers speak to young graduates—and weep!

The adage "He who can, does. He who cannot, teaches" is outworn. Today, those "who can't" find an easier, higher-paying job than teaching. Pension is no longer the drawing card either; there are less hazardous pensions to grow old for in other fields.

Most young teachers enter their classrooms with faith that children will learn, with hope that they will teach them, and with love that will surmount all obstacles. If after a few years they turn heretic to their faith, crying, "These kids are dumb!"; if their hopes fade into admitting, "I can't teach these kids!"; if even their love slips away into the selectivity of "That one's a monster!" we cannot blame the teachers. The very nature of their job turns the classroom against them.

Learning to Think

One basic part of a teacher's job is to make students think. They not only have to learn the facts of the Civil War; they have to learn *why* it started, *how* it might have been avoided, and *who* could have altered its course. Those three-letter words dig deep into the human mind, and deep digging comes hard. A forty-hour week of television does not train the student mind to think; it trains the mind to accept.

Kids today dare a teacher to compete with television, and some are able to do it. One teacher leaps on the desk to illustrate a fight scene from Shakespeare. The kids love it. Another tells jokes. But not all are actors and stand-up comedians; some are merely caring, intelligent teachers. If students concentrate, they learn. But they do not have to concentrate on "Starsky and Hutch," which is more exciting, or on "Laverne and Shirley," which is more entertaining.

As one teacher puts it, "I feel I have to be a vaudeville performer to keep the kids interested."

When the teacher is not onstage but is just a competent teacher, students turn off—and against. How many parents have followed up their children's complaints of "My teacher is boring" with a quick trip to the principal's office? How many have risen in defense of their child against the report card "F" because "the teacher is too tough"?

The most common rationale for undone homework or failed tests brought home to parents is, "My teacher didn't explain." Perhaps the teacher did *not* explain. Many good teachers don't: they give assignments intended to make students find their own explanations. Others may in truth explain poorly, or perhaps students listen poorly. In any case, undone homework is no solution. An angry parent is no solution either. The student's own struggle to find the explanation is.

"Sesame Street" explains. That's what is wrong with most TV; it entertains but does not encourage children to think. And that's one of the reasons why kids fight learning.

They also fight it because TV teaches them that happiness and satisfaction can be found easily and quickly—it's called instant gratification. All a child need do if bored or unsatisfied with one program is switch the channel. This can be done repeatedly without having to deal with the boredom. Children ask, "Shouldn't learning, too, be quick and easy?" Not until society answers with an emphatic "No" will forces begin to gather on the teacher's side.

Learning Responsibility

A second basic part of a teacher's job is to hold students accountable for their decisions. Although young people clamor for independence—"I want to do my own thing"—they do not clamor to be responsible for the outcome of their "thing."

Anne's story is not unique. She loafed through a semester of English in tenth grade, reading little more than the first and last chapters of assigned books, avoiding participation in class. Two days before her final exam, she began leafing through books and trying to pull notes together. By the morning of the exam she was frantic, having slept little the night before. She ate no breakfast, went to school a nervous wreck, took the exam and failed it.

She gave the excuse that she had been sick, and her parents concurred. They had the teacher give her a makeup exam. She failed that too. "The teacher is out to get her," they said.

Anne went off for the summer, got private tutoring, and retook the exam in the fall. This time she passed with a D+.

Anne is in the eleventh grade now, repeating the same performance pattern. Neither she nor her parents enabled her teacher to let her make the connection between loafing all year and failing. It seems like an easy connection to make, but not when the parents shift responsibility away from Anne and onto the teacher. The teacher ends up the villain, unfair and incompetent, while Anne comes out on top as the victim.

Two goals are in conflict: the teacher's—accountability— and the student's—easy success. Until students and parents learn to measure success in terms longer than a semester and more meaningful than marks, the teacher who demands accountability will often be seen as the enemy.

Rewards of Teaching

Unquestionably, life is constant conflict for your child's teachers. Not only do they suffer from the community's social ills, but they may also be blamed for them. They fight in the principal's office *for* their students, and in the classroom *against* them. Teachers often feel personally inadequate and must strive to build confidence in their students. They come to school with their own troubles, a broken heart or a broken marriage, only to spend the day mending the breaks of toys, sentences, and friendships.

There are rewards, however.

Recognition: McGill University uncovered one in the course of studying Montrealers who had risen from the slums to success. The common denominator turned out to be Miss A., whom a significantly large number had had as their first-grade teacher.

Remembrance: Helen MacPherson received a book of poems written by a boy she had taught in sixth grade. "A wild one, he was," she recalled. The inscription read, "I hope you find an echo of your teaching in these poems." She had taught him seventy-one years ago!

Awareness: Kate runs a one-room schoolhouse in Utah. "My special moment came this week when the children were deciding whether to collect money for the Salt Lake City Zoo to 'adopt' an elephant. A second-grader, silent during the discussion, finally said, 'Elephants are so big and I think our school is too small.' It's amazing what happens when we allow our children to think."

It is important for parents to realize that a teacher's joys are few and far between. Not many Miss A.s exist to be recognized; not many students inscribe books of poetry to their teachers; and there are many teachers too busy to be aware. The pains are many and often.

It is important because this is the person who lives with their child six hours a day—perhaps for more waking hours than the parents themselves—and has more of the child's focused interest. Little wonder that young children frequently slip and call a woman teacher "Mother."

This is the person whom you can convince that through team teaching your child can best learn. Who is the other member of the team? You—the parent.

THE PARENT-TEACHER TEAM

A speaker for the National Education Association said recently, "The child who is successful in school usually has parents who are constantly involved with the teacher." Many teachers echo those words.

"I know I can do only half a job," says one, "if the parents aren't interested."

Why would parents not be interested? Many of them are made by the school to feel unwanted; many are afraid, insecure in the area of education. Some are too busy; some think they are too busy. Many care about their children, but as for school, "that's the teacher's job."

The basic fact for you to know in forming a partnership with a teacher for the best possible education of your child is simply this: Your goals are the same.

Parents and teachers at a meeting were asked the same question: "What do you want for these children in school?" The majority of teachers replied, "I want them to reach their fullest potential." Parents answered, "We want them to go as far as possible, to do their best, to grow up happy." They were saying essentially the same thing.

Listening to their answers, one marvels that anything but the closest, most supportive relationship between parent and teacher could ever exist. How could parents make those vicious, gossip-filled telephone calls? How could teachers fill the faculty room with such venom?

They do because one human element slips between the parent-teacher goal: ego.

When I was running a school, I reminded both parents and teachers at the beginning of each school year of the aims and hopes we shared. I spoke of growth above achievement, of discovery over performance, of failure as a positive step in learning. I spoke of the things that we both wanted for the children. They agreed. They sat in the auditorium nodding their heads, smiling, warmed by the humanistic goals toward which their children— our students—were headed.

Each September I felt good about this meeting. "We have parents who understand. We have teachers who care. We'll be able to work together. There are no limits." And each year the parents did understand—until. Until their child had trouble with a teacher.

Laurie's father liked Mr. Allen, until she flunked her biology test. Then came the phone call to me. "Laurie knew the material. I listened to it at home. He didn't mark fairly." Parent and teacher became enemies.

Jason's mother worked closely with Mrs. Trilling in second grade, until the teacher found out that Jason had taken a classmate's camera. Then his mother shouted and withdrew the child from school.

Roger's father tried to get the coach fired when Roger failed to make the football team.

David's mother almost hit the teacher during a conference when she suggested a meeting with the school psychologist to discuss David's outbursts of violence and cruelty.

And each year the teachers did understand until—until a parent pointed out a mistake.

Mrs. Towers liked Anna even though she did poorly in English. One day Anna's mother pointed out that no matter what Anna wrote, Mrs. Towers always gave her a D plus. "You put her in a category," she accused. Mrs. Towers never liked Anna again.

Mr. Rosen could not find a way to make Albert understand equations. Frustrated, he shouted "Dumb" at him in class one day. Albert's parents took him to task, pointing out that name-calling would only reinforce their son's lack of confidence. So defensive was that teacher that Albert had to be transferred out of his class.

Miss Woodward played favorites. She liked Donna Lee and the other middle-class children, ignoring the ethnics and minorities. Resenting her prejudice, Donna Lee's mother confronted her. From then on Miss Woodward made snide remarks to Donna Lee about her "friends."

Every one of these parents and teachers had sat nodding in agreement at the school's opening meeting, concurring with the goals and methods of the school, knowing that these would help the children learn and grow. They knew in their minds. But when they stepped on each other's egos, emotions took precedence over thinking.

Working Through Children's Difficulties

These particular parents and teachers lost a working relationship, but the real losers were the children. For they were deprived of an opportunity to work through a difficulty, to grow from a pain. Had the parents been able to maintain teamwork in the face of trouble, the children would have found support from both sides—support not to make the problem vanish, but to help in coping with it. As it was, the parents kicked the teacher off the teaching team, and each child was left alone to pretend that the problem did not exist.

Instead, as parents you should try to view "trouble with a teacher" not as fighting words but as a learning opportunity for your child. This entails, first of all, being unselfish enough to *let your child suffer*. An "F" in biology hurts; being caught stealing hurts; being put in the "slow" reading class hurts; not making the team hurts; being unable to control yourself hurts. But such things do happen. Children can face them, live through them, and be stronger and more confident in themselves as a result, especially if they have a teacher at school and a parent at home to help.

But when a parent's hostility drives the teacher into an enemy camp, the child cannot accept the teacher's support. When a parent's ego obscures a child's weakness, the child receives no help at home. That child is alone. And isolation hurts far more than an "F"—or any other penalty.

Second, it is important to *detach your ego needs* from your child's education. Mr. Williams is not any less of a banker because his daughter fails biology. Mrs. Silver does not stop being a contributor to the community because her seven-year-old still needs to learn about triangles. The Mortons are not disgraced because their daughter has trouble reading.

Each of these children has a problem to solve. That's what school is for. As one teacher says, "If I had kids with no problems, why would they need me?" Parents might ask themselves the same question.

Teachers and children can work through many difficulties together. Teachers, children, and parents can work through *most* of them. However, all three have to see the difficulty as a challenge, not as a social stigma.

That is where the parent most often falls apart. Instead, face the reality that your child is an individual, with unique strengths and weaknesses. Your child tries or doesn't try; achieves or makes mistakes or falls flat. *But it is the child's choice.* Knowing that will build pride and confidence and the strength to try again.

Although parents knew this at the beginning of the year, the ego-weak parent sees a child fail and covers up the failure to avoid personal embarrassment. The child once again is alone with the shame. But the ego-secure parent sees a child fail and feels pride in the attempt. Parents know that the child will try again, do it differently, learn. The parent stand by the child.

If you follow these guidelines, you will be able to abandon the old defense, "My child—right or wrong—is always right." You will solidify the parent-teacher team, and together you may achieve the goals you share.

Working with the Teacher

It is necessary to point out, to prepare you for the worst when you are doing your best, that teachers too have egos. As human beings, they too find their egos getting in the way. It may have happened to you that an innocent question to a teacher was met with shattering hostility.

You may have asked, "Is there anything I can do to help you with Paul?"

The answer may have been a snarled, "Yes, leave his education to me."

Ouch! You tried. What went wrong? Probably ten years of angry parents—nothing to do with you. Meeting parents' attacks year after year, the teacher has built up defenses.

Parents the teacher confronted previously may have been accusing. "How dare you fail my son?" one may have raged out of overprotectiveness. "*You* should fail; you didn't teach him."

What might the teacher do? Launch a counterattack. "It's impossible to teach a child so pampered at home that he won't do his homework." Touché. The fight is under way.

Or the parent may have struck from another side—against the teacher's need not for success but for control. "Joyce said you assigned *Vanity Fair*. Now that's a bit of a drag, isn't it? I told her she could read the new Irving Wallace instead."

To this the teacher may have responded, "You teach Joyce banking, and I'll teach her English." Again touché.

So by the time you arrived with your amiable and sincere offer of help, the teacher was already conditioned to a hostile reaction. You were different, but the teacher did not know that—yet. Teachers *should* know. They *can* know if they take the initiative and reach out to you first. Perhaps this teacher was too busy or too afraid of a rebuff, maybe just negligent. At any rate, in this case, reaching out is up to you.

That's why it's important for you to introduce yourself not only by name but by intention. "I hope you didn't think I meant to interfere," you might explain as the teacher barks at you. "We are genuinely interested in Paul's education and just thought you might be able to use us in some way."

Most people will respond to such words. A team is formed. You and the teacher have become Paul's allies.

"How do you work with a teacher?" parents ask. "What exactly should I do?" Here are some specifics:

Meet with the teacher on every occasion. At the start of the year, make an appointment to see your child's new teacher (or teachers) just to say, "Hello." This means both parents. For too long the business of a child's education was relegated to the mother. But now the father, as he should, takes an active role. A confusing message reaches the child whose father involves himself in schooling only at report-card time. It comes across as, "School is for women; achievement is for men." Pity the boy or girl who grows up with that sexist attitude in this day and age!

Later in the fall (often on Election Day) the school will have an open house, and you will join the other parents of your child's class at a meeting usually held in the classroom. The teacher will explain the plan for the year, and you will see your child's work to date. Be sure to look through the work folder well enough to discuss it with your child that evening. I know a parent who always writes a note to leave in the folder as a surprise.

Do not ask specific questions about your child. If you do, you bore the other parents, taking time from subjects of general interest to them. You also infuriate the teacher, who is torn between wanting to shut you up and having to be polite. You are there to understand what direction the class is taking, of which your child is only one member.

The way to deal with specific questions about your child is to make an appointment to see the teacher separately. In fact, if a problem has arisen, the teacher may beat you to it and ask you first. Go with an open mind, not with the predetermination that the problem, whatever it is, is the teacher's fault.

Children should be present at such conferences. School, after all, is their business. To omit them is both degrading and inefficient. You can do a little easy role playing to see why. Pretend you have a problem at work about taking overly long lunch hours. Your boss calls your spouse in to discuss the situation; they decide you must eat at your desk for a week in order to repattern yourself. Your spouse returns from the meeting. You, who have been waiting anxiously, leap to open the door. "What did the boss say?"

Who needs the middleman? Not you. Not your child. Children can be talked *with,* not *about.* From that kind of communication they will grow. I have seen the three-way conference work at every level: the high school student who is cutting class, the seventh-grader who won't do homework, the third-grader who hits classmates, even the kindergartener who is afraid to come to school.

The school conference is a constructive way of peeking through windows. You and your child let the teacher see what goes on at home; the teacher, on the other hand, lets you see what goes on at school. Sharing this information, from which both of you would be shut off without the conference, enables the child to appear in full dimension. Paul is not just a student to the teacher; he is not just your little boy to you.

Conferences can also clarify misunderstandings brought about when messages are relayed back and forth by your child. As one wise teacher said to a parent, "I'll only believe half of what George tells me about you if you'll only believe half of what he tells you about me."

On the other hand, participation in a three-way conference requires some preparation and skill, and it's not unusual for both parents and teachers to feel uneasy about the conference when it begins and unsatisfied when it ends. The National School Public Relations Association has published a fifteen-page pamphlet entitled "You Are Invited to a Parent-Teacher Conference" that is full of helpful information. You can obtain a free copy by writing to the National School Public Relations Association, 1801 North Moore Street, Arlington, Virginia 22209.

Be honest with the teacher and your children. It's not going to help your child's education if you tell other people your concerns instead of talking directly with the teacher. If you think the teacher gives too much homework, phoning other mothers will not improve the situation. They don't regulate assignments. Go to see the teacher—with your child. Running to the principal with your complaint seldom accomplishes anything; most principals will ask the teacher to get in touch with you. And since you went right to the boss in the first place, the teacher will have every right to be defensive when you meet.

In these liberated times, parents often get astonishing reports from their children of "what my teacher said."

"She said all girls should take the pill."

"He said church attendance isn't worth anything."

Before you fly off the handle, find out if the teacher really said it—not by asking other parents, not by intimidating your child, but by asking the teacher, with your child present.

"If Cindy thought I said that," the teacher might explain, "we certainly weren't communicating clearly. I thought I said that any girl having sexual relations is better off using a contraceptive."

Or, "Perhaps Larry wasn't listening to the second part. I said that church attendance is meaningless unless we live our religion all week."

If, however—and this could happen—the teacher really has advocated something that you as parents cannot support, you must face this too. Maybe you think the teacher has been less than patriotic, or too liberal in advocating legalization of marijuana, or too conservative in discussing marriage. If you tell your child the teacher is wrong, you undermine the teacher's effectiveness; if you ignore the subject, you undermine your own family's value system.

What do you do? You explain to your child that people are different—that they think and feel differently. The situation provides a learning opportunity to alert your child to the world's diversity.

A parent of a young child explained it this way: "You know how you wear one kind of clothes because that's the way you are, and how Mr. Smith wears another kind because that's the way he is? And you don't have to change over to his clothes, do you? Well, it's the same with attitudes. He has his, and you have yours, and you don't have to change there either."

A parent of a high school student said this: "Your teacher grew up with certain values, just as we all do. Dad and I brought you up with values that work for us as a family. Maybe when you are older and have your own family, you will want to make changes."

Young people can understand if you are direct and honest with them.

Involve yourself in the PTA (or Parents' Association). Being part of the school team means joining and participating in whatever parents' group exists in the school. Although such groups have over the years been predominantly female, men have a great deal to contribute and to receive from involvement, and more and more men are becoming active members.

Parents should realize that the PTA is a channel through which change can take place. There are schools where curriculum has been changed through PTA pressure. In Fairlawn, New Jersey, a principal was removed through PTA pressure. In California, Wisconsin, and Florida, alternative schools were developed in response to PTA pressure. Parents' Associations in several New York City schools were responsible for the introduction of the open classroom into the system.

And, of course, the PTA also engages in many traditional activities. Though some may scoff at the endless bake sales and theater benefits, the science teacher who has been given three new microscopes doesn't laugh. Nor does the English teacher who has been given costumes to stage *Romeo and Juliet*. And your child will take renewed pride and interest to know that his or her parents consider the school important enough for *their* time.

Dealing with Student-Teacher Conflicts

"My teacher hates me!" What parents have not heard that phrase, uttered through pouts, screams, or tears? What do you do now?

First, listen, eliciting the child's perception of the situation. "I'm sure you *think* your teacher hates you" might bring forth additional details.

"What kinds of things does the teacher do to make you feel this way?" This question is sure to work. The child will shout out a list of misdemeanors—if not actual offenses—to make you want to run to the Society for the Prevention of Cruelty to Children.

"Never calls on me . . . picks on me . . . tears my work up . . . pulls my hair . . . sends me out of the room for no reason . . . calls me a liar . . ." and on and on and on.

Listen. Do not comment.

Then urge the child to discuss these feelings with the teacher. An older child, certainly one of high school age, should be able to handle such a meeting without you, if encouraged to go to the teacher and to say something like, "I have a feeling that you just hate me. Do you?"

If your child is afraid to broach the subject, show why it is important: If the teacher's attitude is not changed, the child must learn to live with it. And the teacher cannot change without knowing how the child feels.

"Won't *you* go and say it?" your child may ask.

The answer: "No, your teacher doesn't hate *me.*"

A younger child will need your support in order to share feelings of this kind. Make an appointment as soon as possible for both of you.

When you see the teacher, you face one of two possibilities:

One is that the child is imagining the teacher's hatred. It may turn out to be a rationalization for poor work or an attempt to cover up bad behavior. It may also be that the child needs extra attention. In any case, the teacher has the chance to reassure your child and at the same time gain sufficient insight to work with the child more closely. Once reassured of the teacher's regard and now receiving more attention, a hitherto complaining child should be able to settle down with a positive attitude.

The possibility is that the child is not imagining the teacher's dislike. Perhaps there is no acknowledged reason: The teacher and child may have what we call a personality conflict. Left alone, this can grow to such proportions as to form a wall between the two that prevents all communication. Hate and resentment block hearing. A confrontation of the issue may cut it down to size. It may enable both teacher and student to admit, "We don't have to love each other to get along." Teaching and learning can take place when the relationship is accepted for what it is.

If, however, there is a reason, such as trouble in the classroom, it could be that the teacher wishes the child were in someone else's class—and may feel anger or even hatred toward such a disruptive pupil. Although this possibility may come as a shock to parents, if they are honest they may recall times when they longed to lock little Debbie in her room for a few days or send her off to Grandmother's.

Obviously, in this case parents and child must find out which actions alienate the teacher. Does the child clown around in school? Talk back? Cut class? Sneak out to smoke? Draw dirty pictures on the chalkboard?

Once the problem has been discovered, the next question is,

"What can we do about it?" And "we," you must remember, means three (four, counting parents as two) people involved: parents, student, teacher. The solution may be simple: The child needs firmer guidelines. It may be more complex: The child feels lonely and needs peer acceptance. Or it may involve the intricate, personal anguish of a divorce, death in the family, or feelings of rejection and inadequacy.

Teacher and parents, together with the young person, can either unearth the problem or find a professional who can. Awareness of the problem is the first step in getting help. That help comes when the child feels *important* enough to want to improve and *supported* enough to be able to.

"I hate my teacher!" That is the other familiar cry. How does a parent answer? In much the same way.

First, listen. Find out why your child hates—or is convinced that he or she hates—the teacher.

Next, have the child discuss the problem with the teacher— either with or without you. The conference will follow a similar procedure. The reasons for dislike or imagined dislike will be examined for both the student's and the teacher's perspective, and action will be planned to effect future change.

There is, however, one major difference. Whereas there is no such simple problem as a bad child, there *are* bad teachers. Not bad people, but bad, incapable, uncaring teachers. Your child may be stuck with one of them. Bad teachers, keep in mind, are not simply those who give a child low marks or criticize behavior. They are teachers without zest, teachers who exploit their captive audience for ego-fulfillment, teachers who are too insecure to accept new ideas, teachers too afraid to relinquish authority.

Faced with this horror, you can do three things:

First, you can try to remove the teacher from the school. This entails working with the principal, the superintendent, and probably the Board of Education. They may be unaware, or they may have been waiting for such an opportunity. In either case, removing a teacher takes time, effort, and much documentation. Your child may graduate before the event happens (if it ever does).

Second, you may ask to have your child transferred to another teacher. Chances are, if you have been a cooperative parent and if the school schedule permits, the principal will allow such a change. However, I advise against it—strongly.

By moving a child from one teacher to another, you tell the youngster, "Since you are unable to cope with this we'll take charge." Even though the move is welcome, the message for the child is often, "They must think I am not capable of handling this." Self-confidence begins to shrink, deep inside where no one may even notice.

Far better to take the third course: Let the child remain in the classroom, even with a bad teacher. This way the responsibility is put on your child, with your help, to make the best of it. The message this time is positive: "They know I can cope with this." The child's confidence is strengthened.

Rewards for the Child

There are alternative resources to help a child understand what the teacher does not teach. When John's older sister tutored him to compensate for a weak math teacher in junior high, he found she explained things more clearly than his teacher did. "Gee, and he's grown up and paid and everything," he gasped. John learned an important truth that our society works hard to hide: The young are often as wise as the old.

A bright child with a poor teacher can reinforce classwork independently and come out ahead. A weaker student will need extra help from a parent or other source but can still come out even, academically. Both children, in personal growth and inner strength, will run far ahead of the child switched to another class.

Most psychiatrists agree with Dr. Sheppard Kellam of the University of Chicago, who has studied stress in schoolchildren. "Mastering stressful situations," he says, "children can more easily manage future strains in their lives."

The poet Emily Dickinson said it another way:

> We never know how high we are
> Till we are called to rise.

The good teacher and the supportive parent provide opportunities for children to rise every day, both at school and at home. With understanding of each other's differences and a uniting of each other's goals, they can help children accept these opportunities. In accepting them, children learn. In learning, they teach. And parents, teachers, and young people become teachers and learners together in the ultimate teamwork that is education.

Dear Mrs. Miller:

I am a kindergarten teacher and disagree with your idea that children should be included in school conferences. Suspected learning disabilities or other developmental problems should be discussed with parent and teacher alone. Children should be included only when requested by the teacher.

Mrs. L. K.

Dear Mrs. K.:

I am sorry: I do not agree. The greatest help a parent or a teacher can give a child is, I believe, the ability to face life's realities and to cope with them. Children can accept the fact of a learning disability better than not knowing why they feel different from the other children. Too often, alas, parents and teachers have less courage than the child in meeting facts head-on. In shielding the child, they are really shielding themselves from seeing and feeling the child's pain—and ultimately, their own. In the long run, truth—whatever it is—is less painful than pretense. Certainly a parent and teacher might want to discuss a problem alone at first, but I think children should always be brought in to have the problem explained at their level of understanding and to join in the finding of a solution.

Dear Mrs. Miller:

You always write about the Teacher of the Year. Could you please tell us how to get a teacher nominated for that?

We have a teacher we think should win. Thank you.

Alice, Sue, and Jerry

Dear Alice, Sue, and Jerry:

I love hearing about good teachers, especially from the people whose opinion really counts—students. More power to you . . . and to your teacher. Here is the procedure: Write to the Commissioner of Education in your state capital—you do not even have to know his/her name; ask for information on the Teacher of the Year Program and for all the forms you need to fill out in order to nominate the teacher. Since it gets a little complicated, you might enlist the help of your school principal, your teacher's department chairman, or one of your parents. Then, just follow the rules and hope for the best. If you teacher becomes a state winner, she/he is eligible for the National Teacher of the Year Award. Good luck!

Dear Mrs. Miller:

My husband and I were shocked the other day when our sixteen-year-old daughter came home from school and announced that her guidance counselor had told the girls in her class to all take the pill. We do not approve. What should we do?

The T. G.s

Dear Mr. and Mrs. T. G.:

First of all, check with the guidance counselor, making sure your daughter is in on the conference. It is quite likely she misunderstood what the counselor said; a three-way discussion will set the record straight. If, however, the counselor did actually suggest that all the girls take the pill, I think you have to make it clear to both the counselor and your daughter that you do not approve. Such mass prescribing is totally foreign to good guidance methods. Discuss sexual decision-making with your daughter. Point out the emotional responsibility that comes with a sexual relationship—even with the

pill. Give her contraceptive information. But let her
know that your values do not hold with those of her
guidance counselor.

Dear Mrs. Miller:

Do you have an opinion as to why parents who do the
grumbling about subjects, homework, and topics like sex education, for instance, are the ones who do not attend PTA
meetings? If they did, they could be constructive.

Mrs. F.

Dear Mrs. F.:

My opinion might be unprintable because, like you, I
get frustrated by parents who gossip, complain, and
spread rumors but won't attend PTA meetings. Open dis-
cussion of pros and cons is not only a great learning ex-
perience for parents, it is a great way to make their
school as good as they want it. Nonattending grumblers,
I suspect, are threatened people who are afraid to have
their opinions challenged. I have seen them reached,
however:

1. Have the PTA president phone to find out what
day and what time they can attend a meeting.

2. Send a PTA delegate to their home to discuss
their gripes. Don't approach them by saying they are
wrong; instead, ask their opinion and listen.

Dear Mrs. Miller:

Your advice is always to keep in close touch with the
school over your children's problems. In my case, the school is
not especially happy with my interest, and now I have the title
of "overprotective mother." What do I do?

G. W.

Dear G. W.:

Many parents, without meaning to, miscommunicate
their interest. It comes across as attack. Ask yourself
these questions:

1. Do you include your children in school confer-
ences?
2. Do you acknowledge that they are responsible for
part of the problem?
3. Do you insist that they take the consequences of
their actions?
4. Rather than trying to solve the problem, do you
urge each child and the teacher to solve it together?
5. Do you demonstrate interest in school when there
is no problem?
A "yes" to each question is bound to put you, your
children, and the school on the same team.

Dear Mrs. Miller:
    You always urge parents and teachers to work together.
That's great and I agree. But how can you do it when the only
time parents enter the school door is when they're angry and
want to attack you . . . and when teachers are always on the
defensive. It's not easy being a teacher, you know.

L. P. T.

Dear L. P. T.:
    I know. I was a teacher for eleven years. What's
harder, I was a principal for six. What's harder still, I
have been a parent for over twenty. All I can suggest is
that you keep trying. Urge your principal to set up par-
ent-education courses and parent-teacher workshops. It
is only through this kind of effort that cooperation can
be effected. Also, to share your woes, read a sensitive new
book by a teacher—43 Students, 37 Chairs by Dale Han-
son, published by Warren Green. You'll feel better know-
ing you are not alone in saying, "It's not easy being a
teacher."

Dear Mrs. Miller:
    I am an honors student in high school. My social studies
teacher is a total bore. All he does is give us prewritten notes

on the overhead projector, which we have to copy and memorize. There is never class discussion, just tests on every little date and name. What can be done to save our grades and minds from this class?

T. A. M.

Dear T. A. M.:
Your mind is in your hands, not in your teacher's.
You can use all the methods you wish he would: under-
take a project on your own; investigate in depth an area
that interests you; find original source material to make
the subject come alive; read historical novels of the same
period you are studying. Don't get angry at the teacher
for not assigning all this; assign it yourself. When you
learn to stimulate your own education, you learn a lot
more than social studies; you get ready for lifelong learn-
ing which can save you from business and social bores
who may be a lot worse than your teacher. As for saving
your grades: grit your teeth and memorize those names
and dates. You'll forget them anyway.

Dear Mrs. Miller:
Help! I have a seventh-grade son who is certain all his teachers are out to get him. He seeks to enlist me in his real or fancied confrontations with teachers and school. How do I cope with this?

Mrs. Q. B.

Dear Mrs. B.:
The best way to cope with it is to face it. Make an
appointment for you and your son to meet with the
teacher he claims is out to get him. Do not go alone—be
sure your son is there too. Let him explain how he
feels—you may have to help him along, but do it without
hostility. If the situation is imaginary, the teacher will
give him reassurance. If it is real, the teacher will point
out what your son does in class to elicit trouble.
The next move is up to him. That is a lesson in
accountability.

3/Bringing Learning Home

You are driving down the street. At the crossroad you come to a STOP sign, with no trees or buildings to block your view. You glance quickly from right to left—not a car in sight. You go on through. In the rearview mirror you notice a white car pull out, follow you, overtake you.

"But, officer," you plead. "There were no cars coming." No matter. You get a ticket.

Tomorrow you will stop at the STOP sign.

You are pushing a basket up and down the aisles at the supermarket. No steak any more; it has doubled in price. Cake mix—up 60¢. Lettuce—$1.00 a head. Impossible! Your budget no longer allows such eating. You select a piece of veal breast—you have never prepared it before, but it is inexpensive, and you saw a recipe for it in your cookbook. Forget the cake mix; it is cheaper to bake from scratch. Replace lettuce with a cucumber. You have stayed within your budget.

You are jogging—or using the fan instead of the air conditioner. You are helping your wife through natural childbirth—or your husband through income tax returns. You are reading a magazine article on sex, a newspaper item on China, or a letter from a friend about her recent efforts in pottery.

In each case you are learning. You may not label your activity as such, but that is what you are doing. You learn not to get another ticket. You learn to repattern your food buying. You learn to jog. You learn to conserve energy. You learn the mystery of childbirth and the mastery of government forms. You learn new views about sex and China, and you discover the excitement of making pots.

Every day you send your child to school to learn: reading, writing, arithmetic, a few other subjects, and, with luck, good behavior. You probably do not realize that while *your child* is in school, *you* are also getting an education, but it is happening all the time. The word "educate" comes from the Latin "to lead out of." Your survival, whether it is avoiding a traffic fine or being able to eat for a week, depends on educating yourself. Your personal growth, whether through jogging, reading, or pottery, depends on it too.

Learning, even when we do not plan it, is a lifelong experience. The infant, still wet and screaming, learns about comfort in Mother's arms; learns to scream for food, to hone the instinct to suck for it; learns about masculinity against Father's rough cheek or beard. And soon techniques of manipulation are learned too: "If I pretend to be hungry, they will pick me up."

In the first year, a baby learns more than at any other time. Parents marvel at the process: babies raise their heads, smile, roll over, find their fingers, reach for a toy—every day a new lesson. Parents learn too: how to pin a diaper, what to play, when to let a baby cry. They learn patience and new anxieties. They learn to dream of the future and to love in a new way.

Though the pace slows down, learning continues—through the walking, running, bicycling, and car-driving years; through the needing, reaching out, rebelling, independent years; through colic and college, measles and marriage—until parents are no longer there to see.

Life is a voyage of discoveries. We are explorers, even against our wills at times, in the pursuit of learning.

How strange it seems, then, that we consider school so separate from life! We send our children to school to learn; at home, we feel, they play. We look at college and graduate school as places for education, but at a job as a place for merely earning a living. Yet Eric Hoffer, one of America's great philosophers, is unschooled. Abraham Lincoln attended school for only one year.

Mark Twain, too, understood that learning takes place by merely living. The author of *Tom Sawyer* and *Huckleberry*

Finn announced, "I never let my schooling interfere with my education."

THE MEANING OF LEARNING

One reason people today split learning from living lies in their definition of the word. They limit the meaning of learning. But learning is not narrow; it includes many different kinds.

Skills as One Kind of Learning

The great master Piaget explained that children acquire learning skills in natural sequence; they cannot learn a higher skill before mastering a lower one. In other words, they cannot skip one skill and move on to the next. To understand the relativity of size means to advance in stages. First, for instance, the child must learn to distinguish between a tall, thin jar and a short, wide jar. When the jars are filled with equal amounts of water, it seems that the tall jar holds more. Even if water is poured from the tall jar into the short jar and the tall jar refilled, the child still believes that the tall jar contains more water. The learning level in a child to comprehend that tall and thin can be equal in quantity to short and wide has not yet been reached. It would be useless, and foolish, to try to explain this until later.

But some parents often attempt to force skills before a child is ready to grasp them. Remember the term "reading readiness," when the teacher explained that your child was not yet ready to read, and you got angry because it seemed to you that all the other neighborhood kids of the same age *were* ready? Piaget claims that many parents actually set their children back in kindergarten by forcing the alphabet on them at home and sending them to school unable to tie their shoes. At five some children may not be ready to learn the alphabet; they *are* ready to tie their shoes.

"Back to basics," many parents cry today, demanding that the curriculum be changed, methods reversed, alternative schools staffed. They want more attention paid to the three R's—and well they should, for many schools, in their well-intentioned efforts to broaden their base, have let the three R's slide.

It is preposterous, however, to assume that *including* the three R's necessitates *excluding* other lessons to be learned.

Unfortunately, in shouting about basics, these parents apparently don't stop to ask, "Basic what?" Reading, writing, and arithmetic are not the only basics; they are simply three obvious and well-publicized ones. Unfortunately, schools responding to the "Back to basics" cry too often overreact, abandoning other basics in the sweep.

There are many basic skills that need to be learned:

Survival skills. Studies of health, nutrition, environment, consumer awareness—these are skills. Knowing the community and working with it is a skill. Understanding politics is a skill. For many, typing, cooking, auto mechanics, computer operations, and farming are basic skills. Unfortunately, the dual pressures of budget cuts and "Back to basics" have eliminated most of these skills from the general curriculum.

Skills of pleasure. What joy to learn the skill of using one's body—to bat a single, to serve an ace, to swim a crawl, to flip from the parallel bars! What fulfillment to play the piano, accompany yourself on the guitar, paste a collage, dance, write a poem, act Lady Macbeth! How satisfying to weave a basket, develop a photograph, build a cabinet, tool a leather briefcase! Here too are skills to be learned—athletics, arts and crafts—skills to enrich a whole life. Yet they have been the first courses to be tossed out to save money or to make room for "basics."

Thinking skills. Using the mind is a skill. But few high schools offer courses in philosophy or logic or problem solving; in fact, few demand more than rote memory of their students. Yet parents rarely complain that their children are not learning how to think.

As early as kindergarten and all through the grades, children can be taught to analyze. It begins with asking the right questions:

"Jason threw a toy at Maria. What reasons did he have?"

"Mrs. White says no unexcused absences. What arguments might change her mind?"

"Dad is so old-fashioned. What are his fears about my generation?"

From kindergarten and up, children can be taught to draw conclusions too:

"If I hit Will, he will probably hit me back, and it will hurt."

"The teacher was mad at me all day. Maybe I shouldn't come in late again."

"Life will be calmer if I obey the rules and come home at eleven P.M., like Mom and Dad said."

Asking questions and making connections—that is thinking. Yet, in all the screaming for fundamentals, I hear few voices raised to add a big T to the three R's.

Personal skills. The most intense joys in life come through our personal relationships: parent-child bonds, friendships, co-working teams, love affairs, sex partnerships, marriage. The most intense pains stem from the same source: torn relationships, with their feelings of rejection, indifference, rebellion, anger, and sense of failure.

For a few years schools and parents were aware of the need to teach personal skills to children—affective education, it was called. But people misunderstood; they thought that including personal skills meant *excluding* the three R's, so they pulled back. Reactionaries echoed the sentiments of California's former Educational Commissioner, Max Rafferty: "We're stressing such intangibles as the happy acceptance of the child by his peer group, relevance, inward motivation, and all that junk! We've got away from the basics and fundamentals."

Those schools that responded by allowing extra three-R's drilling to replace communication skills and affective learning may have raised reading scores a point or so (*may have,* mind you), but they may also be producing a group of one-dimensional people. Here is the irony: Tests prove that children who are participating in a *full* learning situation learn to read and write better. The reactionaries of the world defeat their own purpose.

Information as Another Kind of Learning

Parents are accustomed to judging their children's progress in school by test scores and report cards. Alas, so are teachers to a large degree. Most tests are based on "what the child has learned this marking period." A student who has been able to write three reasons for the oil shortage as explained by the teacher or to name three kinds of short stories as explained by the textbook or to list three kinds of saltwater fish as found in the encyclopedia will receive a sure A.

A great deal of information is imparted in school—usually from teacher to student. Sometimes more meaningful is the information passed from student to student, either openly or secretly in the lavatory. Occasionally, a miracle occurs, and information is passed from student to teacher, but for this to occur takes a truly mature mind—on the part of the teacher, that is. Students impart information every day, but we usually don't accept it.

I don't mean to belittle information per se; your children can pick up facts in school that will serve them all their lives. Shopping at the supermarket will be speedier because they memorized the multiplication tables. Reading the daily newspaper will have more meaning because they learned the capitals of Egypt, Iran, and Russia.

But stop and ask yourself how many facts you learned in school that were important to you beyond that particular classroom. What facts are important to you now? Which do you even remember?

It is, rather, the information we learn about processes that stays around to help us. Your child need not remember the characters and plot of the novels studied in school, such as *Treasure Island,* in order to enjoy an adult novel later on. What Robert Louis Stevenson did with his material, rather than the material itself, enriches adult reading of authors as varied as Jane Austen and Kurt Vonnegut. Similarly, a chemistry student need not remember that the residue of sodium chloride weighed a certain number of grams in an experiment in order to understand the scientific process.

Teachers would do well to put more emphasis on the content of their courses as a *means,* not as an *end,* to learning. Parents would do well to worry less about how much their children are stashing away in their brains and more about how they are applying it.

Most lawyers know how to put facts in their proper place.

The lawyer's bookshelf is lined with tomes, the contents of which may have been memorized on demand in law school but which surely have been forgotten by now. However, the lawyer can quickly locate the right volume to solve a client's problem, having retained the needed "how-to" information. Many clients might feel, in fact, that the lawyer could have used the memorization time in law school to better advantage by learning more about human behavior and feelings instead.

Education should take a lesson from the lawyer. It is far less vital, for example, that your son know details of the lives of America's great men than that he know where and how to find those details. It will be of far greater value to your daughter to know how to use a table of valences than to spend time memorizing them. Learning to use a dictionary, a computer, and a typewriter could help students who are bogged down hopelessly in spelling, multiplication tables, and script.

Schools are in the business of imparting information. Agreed. They need a redirection of that focus, however, and they need parental clout to help them move. So instead of quizzing for facts, try asking your children some thought-provoking questions and see what happens.

A suburban father did just that. "Forget your six economic categories," he said to his son while helping him study for an exam. "Tell me what reasons a person might have to try to change them."

He was stunned by his son's response, which came with not a moment's hesitation: "Come on, Dad. We don't have to know that for the test."

Some wise man once said that the aim of education is to turn a child's mind into a fountain, not into a reservoir. Parents and teachers ought to heed his words. Of course, children need to master the three R's, but not at the expense of the vast areas of learning that lie beyond. Reading, writing, and arithmetic are merely means of transportation to that learning.

HOW LEARNING TAKES PLACE

Now that we know what a multifaceted process learning really is, another question arises: What makes it take place?

Learning happens when there is need. A baby learns to scream because of a need to communicate hunger or a wet bottom. A child learns to talk after reaching a certain level of frustration over less efficient means of communication. A teenager learns to drive when he or she wants Dad's car and doesn't want to be driven by Dad. You learn to stop at STOP signs when you want to avoid a ticket. In educational jargon the word is motivation, but it is just plain old need.

The apocryphal story of a ten-year-old boy who had never spoken a word illustrates the point. His worried parents had taken him all over the United States for help, to no avail. One morning at breakfast, sipping his cocoa, he yelled, "Dammit. That's hot!"

His parents stared. "You can speak," they gasped.

The boy nodded.

"Why haven't you spoken before?"

The boy replied, "Everything was all right until now."

In other words, when everything is all right, there is no need to reach out and learn. That may be one reason so many students are turned off by school. Another is irrelevance. The ghetto boy sees no reason for learning to read words in standard reading books—words like "ranch house," "father," "lawn," and "family." They aren't useful—not in *his* life. Smart educators are beginning to rewrite books, using words from the ghetto world: "garbage," "empty lot," "street," and "apartment." With such a vocabulary, this boy is more likely to learn to read.

At the other end of the socioeconomic scale is the suburban boy who hates school, posh and expensive as it may be, because he wants to be an auto mechanic. Why, he wonders, does he have to wade through physics and ancient history? He has to, that's all—because his school demands it and his parents expect it. Finally, a teacher may reach him and explain that the math he learns in school can help him become a good auto mechanic; the history he studies can enable him to understand more of the current world scene; English and art and music can build inner resources to ensure him against boredom. This makes sense, and he studies enough to get through school. That teacher understands how to reach him at the level of *his* need, not the *school's,* and thereby saves him from total rebellion.

You can do what that teacher does by looking at the situation the way your child sees it. Nagging will not lead to study, nor will threatening: a child sees these as calls to battle. What will get results is seeing that school can help do what matters. Maybe your son wants to sail; math is important in navigation. Maybe your daughter wants to travel abroad; a foreign language makes it more fun. Maybe your child wants to make a lot of money; a college degree enhances that chance. Maybe he or she just wants to get out of high school and be free; children need passing grades to graduate.

Too many parents consider personal growth off limits for school, just as they consider academic growth off limits for home. But the girl watching her father balance a checkbook or her mother measure ingredients for a cake is learning math as surely as though she sat in class. On the other hand, the boy experiencing sexual curiosity along with Holden Caulfield as he studies *The Catcher in the Rye* is getting more real sex education than he would in a talk with his parents.

Learning takes place everywhere. It cannot be compartmentalized any more than people can be, with certain places assigned and labeled for certain lessons. The great debate about sex and values education in school is pointless. The question is not *whether* children learn sex and values there; they *are* learning those things no matter what we do. The question is *how* they will learn them. Teachers and parents can only hope to guide that learning.

What are parents who fight sex education in the classroom going to do about sex education at the newsstand and in the movies and in the back seat of the car? What are parents who say values teaching belongs in the home going to do about children who cheat to get better grades or talk behind a friend's back or lie to a teacher?

Learning goes to school even without parental consent.

The argument over whether children should learn "school subjects" at home is equally pointless. They *are* learning them—every time parents answer, or refuse to answer, a question. How is the teacher to overcome negative attitudes at home or those that breed self-hatred or the belief "that girls don't need to be educated," for instance?

Learning is brought home without an invitation.

Who, then, is the real educator? Is it the teacher or the parent? Buckminster Fuller answers, "Education must be done by yourself—nobody can give it to you."

Parents rarely grasp this point. They attack the teacher who "doesn't explain" and prod the child who "won't do homework." Many parents overorganize the lives of their children to make sure they will be given the proper lessons—ice skating, tennis, dancing, skiing, singing, and gymnastics. Schools and summer camps abound, giving specialized training to America's children. I look back with longing at the little overalled boy carrying his fishing pole and a can of worms down the road, learning to fish alone.

Most teachers fail to grasp Buckminster Fuller's point, too. How upset they get if Jerry leaves early to attend a matinee with his family. How irate if Betsy misses class once a week to tutor a second-grader. And can forgiveness ever come if Bill cuts the last week in June to go to Europe? Of course, parents should not disrupt a child's schedule regularly. I am not advocating that. But if something exciting is happening outside the four walls of the classroom, a parent should be able to take the child out without wails and moans from the teacher.

Students also misunderstand, reflecting the views of their parents and teachers. "Teach me," they demand. Richard Donahue sued his school for not teaching him to read. Others followed suit. They lost. Not only did the court find their case unfounded; so did some of their peers. As a young man wrote to the *New York Times,* "You can't teach a kid who is looking out the window." That young writer knows that if he gets an education, he has to reach for it. Perhaps in time he will learn that he can do it even while looking out the window.

For outside the window lies the world. Children watch television, hear the radio, ride in airplanes, and think about rockets; they read newspapers, observe politicians in action, and get to vote before long; they go to movies and dream about the future. The world beyond that window is vibrating with stimuli far more exciting than those in the classroom.

Marshall McLuhan was aware of this when he wrote, "The world pool of information fathered by electric media far surpasses any possible influence mom and dad [or teacher] can now bring to bear.... Education is no longer shaped by only two fumbling experts. Now all the world's a sage."

This being so, where is the young person's education to begin? Where is it to end?

Not within the four walls of a school.

The studies of Christopher Jencks and James Coleman point out the strength of parents as teachers, but few teachers should need proof of this. For they can see for themselves how the child reflects the home. When Willy Black, the 1979 National Teacher of the Year, was asked what makes a good student, she said, "Coming from a home where there are opportunities to pursue varied interests and parents who are interested in lots of things."

Although teachers are aware of this parent power, parents themselves sometimes seem less conscious of it. They feel free to criticize what a teacher *is* doing, but loath to undertake what he or she is *not* doing. But when they do switch from a passive to an active role, not only do their children benefit through better learning, but they themselves can find new interests and lose old frustrations.

HOW YOU CAN EXTEND EDUCATION

There are many ways in which parents are able to extend their children's classroom at any grade level.

Teaching by Example

Learning is brought home by parents even before they undertake it consciously, for you teach by being what you are. Your children copy you—not always by intention, but often by assimilation. Statistics show the close correlation between parents who read and children's reading activity, between parents who abuse their children and those children who grow up to become abusing parents, between alcoholic parents and young people who drink heavily, between overweight parents and overweight children.

We're all aware of the close correlation between parents

who play with their children and children who can play, between parents who are athletic and sports-minded children, between parents with interests and interesting children. Haven't you yourself acknowledged the correlation when you have said things like, "No wonder Suzy can't spell. I can't either!" Or, "Larry has his father's temper."

Even during the adolescent years when children normally rebel against parental values in their quest for independence, the strength of parental example is at work: They usually react smack against it. The son of a gray-suited Madison Avenue account executive may grow a beard and wear shirts with holes in the elbows. The daughter of the town's most Victorian family may earn the reputation of the wildest girl in school.

Example being the pervasive teacher it is, parents ought to do some serious self-examining to determine the kind of example they are setting. Here are a few of the kinds of questions you might want to ask yourself:

1. Does my child see me reading books—for pleasure, not just for work?
2. Does my child see me work hard at my job—not slack off when I am tired or want a few extra vacation days?
3. Does my child see me tell the truth—even when I want to avoid an invitation?
4. Does my child see me willing to pay the price of honesty—even on my income tax?
5. Does my child see me put less emphasis on money, clothes, and the house than on people?
6. Does my child see me giving to others—not just in money but in time and concern?
7. Does my child see my spouse and me express affection and respect for each other?
8. Does my child see my spouse and me talking together, instead of spending all our time at work or watching television?
9. Does my child see that I am excited about outside interests?
10. Is my child aware that my love makes me say "No" sometimes, yet is aware of being accepted, failures and all?

If you can answer a truthful "Yes" to these ten questions, you can rest assured that your child is learning the right lessons by example.

While going over these questions with a mother a few months ago, I saw her lose her temper at her six-year-old son, who was screaming for her attention.

"Stop shouting at me!" she shouted at him.

I looked at her and then at the little boy, both of whom burst out laughing. That, too, was learning by example.

Teaching by Exposure

Learning is also brought home by parents when they surround their children with stimuli conducive to growth: books, things to make, paints, good music, scales, measuring tapes, clay, sewing, and plenty of conversation. One of the major concerns of social scientists who study the education of the disadvantaged has been that parents of slum children spend too little time with them and provide too few positive stimuli. They themselves are often so lacking in educational background that they may not be able to communicate the values of learning to their children. As a result, many of their children grow up repeating their pattern.

The Head Start Program was developed to deal with this problem by providing at early childhood learning centers the prelearning experiences not found in these homes. Kindergarten and primary teachers reported increased curiosity and receptivity to learning among preschoolers in the program. There seemed indications at last of hope for success in the battle to upgrade the education of disadvantaged children. Unfortunately, the program did not provide for follow-up support of the Head Start children as they moved into elementary school. And like many innovative programs, it became a victim of the cutback in federal funds for education and was abandoned in many areas within a few years.

At the other extreme, children in affluent schools can also be deprived. Given *things* instead of *attention*, they are frequently denied experiences necessary for growth.

What are these experiences, and how can you expose your

children to them? One of the simplest ways is to take walks to-gether; as you walk, *look*. City families can point out to each other what they see: new architecture, an old cobblestone street, an ethnic quarter with foreign food, clubs and movie houses, a neighborhood fair, a tiny park, window boxes with flowers, crafts stores, some streets neatly kept and others strewn with garbage, people. They can identify and count the different na-tionalities of restaurants, the breeds of dogs, the bus lines, the kinds of museums. They can look at and talk about the diversity that makes up a city.

Rural families, too, can walk and see: shapes of trees and the variety of wild flowers, lines of the horizon and contours of the hills and meadows, wild berries, animals and insects that scurry by, birds and the sound of their calls, snow changing na-ture's shapes, roads and airplanes, boats if they live by the wa-ter, and water itself.

While you customarily walk in your own community, per-haps you can go farther afield at times. The country family can walk in the city and the city family in the country—what new worlds are to be discovered by each!

Inside, too, you can expose your children to causes of won-der, which, by the way, poet Carl Sandburg calls "the highest to which man can attain." There is the miracle (not to mention the smell), of rising bread, of Dad's office on a rainy day, of Moth-er's jewelry box. There is the fun of pulling taffy, of building a secret place under the dining room table, of modeling with clay. And there are unknown worlds to be discovered in books of art and travel, in almanacs and atlases. There are scrapbooks of leaves and trains and fishes to be pasted, there are the beauty and joy of music, and then there is the magic to be found in mo-ments of quiet.

These stimuli are available to all parents. You cannot, how-ever, merely gather them in around your child and say, "Learn." Children, especially young ones, need to be led to the edge of discovery. One mother gave her children a box of seashells that she treasured. To her they were the miracle of nature; to her children they were curiosities to hold their attention only a few minutes. But when the mother explained that at one time tiny animals had inhabited them, the children came alive, spending the rest of the day trying to figure out who had lived within—and how. Parents have had similar experiences with stamps and coins.

No matter how bad the school or how dull the teacher, you as a parent have the power to keep your child's mind curious and creative. As long as you are exciting, your child will be excited; as long as you are stimulating, your child will be stimulated to learn.

Teaching by Sharing

Today more than half of the mothers of school-age children in America hold full-time jobs, and almost all the fathers do. Both may come home late, tired, with household chores to do. "Where," they ask, "are there hours to share with our children?"

But the hours *are* there, somewhere. Maybe they can be found trading off an afternoon golf game or a quiet cocktail hour or a Saturday morning of housework. The important thing is to find them. The personal growth that both parents and children gain from shared hours is exceeded only by the growth in their relationship.

How do you turn sharing into learning? You might begin with television, which the average child watches up to forty hours a week in America—more hours than are spent in school.

Preschool children should have their television censored by parents; they are not yet able to put what they see in perspective, nor are they aware enough to discuss with their parents the messages they're getting from TV. But school-age children are more mature, and I truly believe that there is nothing on television that can harm them *if* they and their parents watch it together, discussing it as they watch.

It's important, though, for parents to stop using the machine as a baby-sitter, tempting as it is sometimes, in order to gain a few hours of quiet for themselves. One good approach is to allow each member of the family to select a show to be watched by everyone together. Just the process of taking turns teaches a child selectivity. Watching adult shows the parents choose broadens youthful interests. And introducing parents to the child's television world imparts a feeling of importance.

If you have not already succumbed, I urge you not to give your children their own television sets. This is one admonition that I cannot deliver strongly enough, because a child glued to a favorite program in the bedroom is isolated from the family, and the home becomes a series of individual cells rather than a group entity. An alternative would be for parents to put off private conversations or the reading of the evening paper until after the children's bedtime so that more time can be spent together. If the television is to be on for their children, they should join them in watching it.

If my warning comes too late and your children are well into solo televiewing in their rooms, I urge you to make an all-out effort to reshape their habits. Invite them into the living room to watch with you; they may be flattered enough to accept. If not, ask whether you may watch with them in their rooms; they may be too stunned to refuse. Actually, children like to be with their parents when they come together on an equal footing; if you take turns selecting programs, you and they can abandon rank and simply enjoy watching a show together. Sharing a program is more fun than watching it alone. With a little imagination, you can make your children prefer family viewing on most nights, providing you are willing to sacrifice some of your favorite shows in favor of theirs. When they have friends over, though, you can let them opt for privacy.

There are some wonderful TV shows to watch together: theater, opera, ballet, nature explorations, the circus, news. There are entertaining shows as harmless and as much fun as "Barney Miller." And there are the kind some of us find hard to take, such as "Charlie's Angels" and "Bionic Woman"; if your children choose to watch one of these shows when their turn rolls around, try to grin and bear it.

A current Harvard study reveals that parents and children discuss sex no more openly today than they did before the so-called sex revolution. Parents continually report that they worry over their children's viewing of blood and gore, as well as sex, on television, but they do not know what to do about it. The answer is to *watch and discuss together*.

"But I don't know what to say," a mother admits timidly. The following questions are offered as aids to initiating discussion. You will probably think of a hundred more as you and your child watch a TV show.

1. Do you know anyone who acts like that person?
2. If you acted like that at home (at school), what do you think would happen?
3. Have you ever been in a similar situation?
4. What do you suppose that person is feeling?
5. Is there another way he or she could have solved that problem?
6. How does it make you feel?
7. Would you want any of the people in the show for your friends?
8. Why do you think people like to watch this show?
9. How could this show be more interesting? More realistic?
10. Would you want a small child to watch this show?
11. What effect do you think the show would have on troubled kids?
12. What is the show really saying? Do you believe it?
13. What would you say the goal of that character is?
14. Whose side are you on?
15. What is scary about that?
16. Does that look like fun?
17. Do you think they love each other?
18. Would you handle anger in that way?
19. On a scale from 1 to 10, how do you rate this show on importance? Acting? Writing?
20. How does the advertising make you feel?

And so on and on and on. One question could trigger an evening's discussion.

Aside from television, there are other areas in which you and your children can share, and thereby learn. Reading, for instance, can be a shared experience. I know a family that has what they call "A Night Aloud." Several evenings a week a family member selects a passage from a book or poem or a scene from a play, reads it, then leads a discussion about it. This is an entertaining, creative way to share an evening. Another way to share reading would be to have each member read a book and then report on it. Or try this: Each family member could take a newspaper headline as a topic for dinner conversation, sharing their opinions with others in the family. Some families go further—they enroll in a course together, learning a craft or a sport at the local Y, high school, or community college. Others undertake a family project—to build a porch, learn to hike, or make Christmas gifts.

Some towns offer parent-child centers developed for the express purpose of sharing learning experiences. There is something called the Parent/Child Toy Library springing up in different cities, where families play together with games designed for learning. There is the Exploratorium in San Francisco, where 450 exhibits invite parents and children to discover. Vassar College offers a weeklong preschool parent-child shared work and play experience, which is aimed at stimulating similar experiences at home.

With help or alone, parents can become skilled at sharing with their children the opportunities for growth that school does not—and cannot—provide.

Teaching by Guiding

Older children require fewer shared activities with their parents. In fact, they accept fewer activities because they are beginning to pull away, and they prefer sharing with their peers. The parent role, then, becomes one of guiding your son or daughter toward opportunities that extend learning.

By the time children are twelve or thirteen, they should be able to carry through a project on their own. They can undertake an independent study on any subject that interests them—from astronauts to zodiac signs. Good teachers encourage students to develop home projects evolving from schoolwork. For instance, ancient history can spin off an independent study of myths, of architecture, or of religion. Biology can spur pursuit of genetics or tests on the circulatory system or a study of plants.

In the absence of such an encouraging teacher, a parent

may serve the same purpose, being careful only to suggest, not to prod or do the work for the child. Remember to give what every good teacher gives—feedback. Children respond with renewed vigor when parents are honestly interested, when they want to hear what the children are doing and even go so far as to ask questions.

Parents wise enough and caring enough to guide their children into being their own teachers can help them acquire mental and emotional maturity for life.

Teaching by Using the Community

Opportunities for learning in the community are limitless. However, unless parents use them themselves or at least point them out to their children, they may pass unnoticed.

Cities, towns, and rural areas in America abound in learning resources. It may be museums as grand as Washington's Smithsonian Institution or as tiny as Stamford's Historical Society. It may be a zoo or a costume collection or Cleveland's display of antique cars. It may be an Indian museum in Colorado, Sarasota's Circus Museum, or California's Hearst mansion. In upper New Hampshire it is boxes of hands-on arts and artifacts delivered to out-of-the-way classrooms on demand. By exploring, parents may discover all kinds of specialized learning centers in their community and nearby.

They may discover surprises at their libraries as well, for libraries are not just for books any more. They often offer courses, lectures, other kinds of programs; they also provide records and, in many cases, musical instruments.

Local high schools and colleges should not be overlooked. Many of them have offerings for the teens as varied as typing, boat safety, sewing, lifesaving, and balancing a checkbook.

While you are studying these possibilities within your community, you should also consider opportunities for volunteer work. Hospitals need candy stripers; the blind need readers; schools need tutors; neighborhoods need street sweepers and flower tenders; nursery schools need aides; cable TV stations need gofers; political headquarters need envelope sealers.

I have seen youngsters no older than twelve brighten lives

in an old-age home with their weekly visits. I have seen a ten-year-old relieve a blind man of daily marketing. I have seen teenagers bring warmth to the deaf and the mentally retarded, without which their lives would have been a prison.

In each case the service rendered filled a crying need that would otherwise have gone unheeded. The receiver was aware and grateful. It was the giver, however, who made the real gain, not only by learning the habit and the joy of giving, but also by realizing that he or she had something valuable to give.

Here, then, are five ways in which you as a parent can extend your children's learning. They are so obvious you may have gasped when you read about them, so easy you almost disbelieved. Above all, they are such fun that you may wonder whether this can be learning. Yes, for that's what learning is!

The world into which the student looks and dreams glimmers sunlight. The teacher's lowering of the blinds cannot blot it out, for school is too confining for the life adventure of learning. The world itself must be a schoolroom, and the world begins at home. You can raise the blinds for your child.

All you need is time, which you can find when you know how important it is to use it in this way.

All you need is awareness, which dawns when you realize you have been your child's teacher since birth.

All you need is faith, which you cannot deny when you see your child grow.

Your job is done—and well done—when you have opened the doors to the world and guided your child through them, equipped to cope with what comes.

Shakespeare's Cardinal Wolsey in *Henry VIII* says to Lord Cromwell as they part for the last time:

> When I am forgotten, as I shall be,
> And sleep in dull cold marble ...
> Say, I taught thee.

Every parent can earn the right to say the same. For the ultimate bequest parents leave is the person their child has become.

Dear Mrs. Miller:
The Teacher of the Year may be terrific, but the teachers
my children have couldn't care less. Reading, writing, and
arithmetic, and their job is done. Isn't there more to education
than that?

Mrs. Emma L.

Dear Mrs. L.:
Yes, there is. Let Bill Zepka, principal of Groveton
Elementary School in Alexandria, Virginia, answer you:
"Remember, the teacher has your child for only 30
hours out of the 168-hour week. If you hold the teacher
accountable for those 30 hours, how many of the remain-
ing 138 are you accountable for? Ten hours of sleep a
day? One half hour of homework nightly? Fifteen minutes
of daily reading? Fifteen minutes of talking and listening
to one another? That still leaves you with more than
twice the hours that the teacher has. Are you using them
wisely? Think about it before casting the first stone."

Dear Mrs. Miller:
Our seventh-grade son has recently undergone a back operation that will keep him out of school for several months. He
is an earnest kid and worried about missing so much school, as
we are also. What do you think we should do?

Mr. and Mrs. S. A. E.

Dear Mr. and Mrs. E.:
In most states, a school district is required to pro-
vide home instruction for children in situations similar
to yours. It costs no money and is available for all chil-
dren—even those attending private school. I suggest you
contact the Superintendent of Schools in your district
and find out what can be arranged for your son. No mat-
ter what the school provides, however, remember that
you will have to give a great deal of encouragement and

support. Try to bring some of the fun part of school home to him, too. Let his friends come to report social doings. Keep art supplies handy. Tape school plays and musical programs so that he can share them. Take photographs of athletic events. He will return to school feeling he hasn't missed all that much.

Dear Mrs. Miller:

Do you believe that parenting courses should be taught to parents by elementary and secondary schools? And if so, what would you teach?

P. V.

Dear P. V.:

Yes, most heartily, yes! Anyone who works with children sees immeasurable damage done to them by their parents—parents who love them, parents who mean well ... but, alas, parents who do not know any better. Raising children takes both love and skill; the latter can be taught. I would include the following in an adult parenting course: 1. How to help your child feel good about himself. 2. How to discipline creatively instead of merely punish. 3. How to work with the school for your child's better education. 4. How to help your child build inner resources. 5. How to instill moral values. These are not easy lessons to learn, but parents can acquire skills and develop insights which enable them to do a better job of child rearing. It is a wise school that offers a course or even a seminar in parenting. And it is the wise parent who attends.

Dear Mrs. Miller:

Does every state offer programs for the gifted child? How do I go about finding out what to do for mine?

J. A. D.

Dear J. A. D.:

No, I regret to say that very few states have mandated programs for the gifted child. Since educational regulations change rapidly, there is no point in my telling you what your state has; it may no longer have it by the time you read my answer. Instead, contact the Commissioner of Education in your state capital and ask the question. If your state mandates programs for the gifted, you are fortunate; your child will receive a good education—even if the state has to pay for attendance at a private school. If your state doesn't offer gifted programs, start putting pressure on your legislators and on the Commissioner. In addition, try to work out an individualized program with the school. Finally, read a wonderful new book called The World of the Gifted Child *by Priscilla Vail. She offers lots of help.*

Dear Mrs. Miller:

I dread the thought of having my teenage daughter home all day during the summer. She is too young to work and too old to follow me around. We can't afford to send her to camp. Does the summer have to be agony for all of us?

Anonymous Mother

Dear Anonymous:

Though nameless, you are honest and share your dread with anonymous mothers throughout the country. No, summer can be wonderful with a teenager. Turn it into a time for learning life skills—those bits of knowledge that the adults she probably envies find themselves needing most of the time. Let her . . . and him too . . . learn to cook. If there aren't courses available, teach her yourself or get a do-it-yourself book. How about sewing? Carpentry? Growing vegetables? Raising animals? Let her redecorate her room—paint, build shelves, make drapes, etc. Or let her fix up the basement. Let your teenager learn to swim, take a lifesaving course. Let her learn typ-

ing, maybe shorthand. Help her outline an independent study course in newspaper reading or shopping within a budget or banking or writing checks. Give her a share of stock—it may cost no more than $10 to $20—and let her learn about investments. Teenagers are learners and doers by nature. Let your teenager learn and do her way through the summer. If you are lucky, you'll be learning and doing along with her.

Dear Mrs. Miller:

Our family has an opportunity to go abroad this summer for three months in several different countries. Of course, we are bouncing with excitement. The only drawback is that our children in third and fifth grades will miss four weeks at the beginning of the school year. How bad is that going to be for them?

Mrs. A. B.

Dear Mrs. A. B.:

Not nearly so bad as missing out on the growth experience that travel brings. Go on your trip—have fun—and don't worry. See and talk about everything with your children. Take note of customs different from ours. Study Berlitz books and help the children learn phrases they can use in different countries. Take them to parks and let them play with other children. Even let them watch TV so they can hear the language spoken. Before leaving on your trip, however, alert the school principal to the fact that the children will be entering late in the fall. Then speak to the teachers they will have next year—be sure the children are with you. Ask them for work you can take along with you. Tuck it away until September. Then set aside a couple of hours a day on a scheduled basis during which you will supervise the children's assignments. When they return to school, they will be caught up on work and—lucky kids—way ahead in living!

4/Communicating with Your Child

"Bill and I have a great relationship," Mr. Glasser boasts to a neighbor one Saturday afternoon.

"How can you tell?" asks the neighbor as he leans on his lawn mower, hoping for words of encouragement to apply to his own son.

"The main thing is we talk," Mr. Glasser answers. "That's how I know. Bill and I have great conversations."

Halfway across town in John Nutley's basement, Bill Glasser sprawls in front of the stereo. "Do you and your dad ever talk? I mean *really* talk?" he asks.

John shrugs. "Nah."

"Us either. He thinks we do, but we just make words. We don't talk."

"Yeah. I know," John agrees.

Mr. Glasser is not lying to his neighbor. As far as he is concerned, he and Bill do have great conversations. He talks to Bill about polishing the car; he reminds him when a term paper is due; he explains why he should help his mother in the kitchen. He talks to Bill a lot.

And each evening when he returns from work, he pats Bill on the shoulder and asks, "What did you do in school today?"

And each evening Bill responds to that question, "Nothing." To his father, that response does not mean he's not listening. And the fact that Mr. Glasser has settled down to watch the news on TV does not mean he's not listening either. Mr. Glasser is truly oblivious to the fact that he and his son do not talk. Why, he even believes they communicate!

Despite our evolutionary progress, we poor humans cannot come close to the communications efficiency of animals—perhaps because we are called on to communicate abstract thoughts and feelings, while animals send more concrete instinctual messages. We have technology from the Morse Code to Telstar and beyond, but we still cannot seem to tell one another what is on our minds. Animals can. Ants are blind, but they indicate where they are through a scent that sends no garbled messages. Bees make no vocal sounds, but a wiggle dance that they perform announces the whereabouts of a pollen find loud and clear. A female peacock has no doubts as to the male's message when he fans that marvel of colored tail before her. Animals thump, bark, meow, honk, and trumpet, all making indefinite sounds far more intelligibly than we humans sometimes do with all our nuances of language.

In fact, we seem to communicate best when we do not talk. For example, Bill's father is far more interested in how the car is polished than in what Bill did in school today. His routine question does not fool Bill. Something probably did happen in school—it nearly always does—but he is not about to tell his father. "Nothing" spares him.

As Eric Hoffer, self-proclaimed philosopher of the working class, phrased it, "Sometimes it seems that people hear best what we do not say."

Parents are far less adept at hearing the unspoken than their children are, as Bill heard his father. Parents settle for words, not hearing what is being said in silence. No wonder. If it is difficult to understand what your child says openly, is it not impossible to understand what he or she does not even express? No, not impossible. Just very hard—and it takes some translating.

A look at three children who have just returned from school may help to make this clear.

The first one slams the front door, screaming, "I hate those kids in my class. They are so dumb, I wish they'd all drop dead in their sleep!"

Her mother races downstairs, scolding. "Why are you always so angry? What a thing to say about your friends! Go to your room until you can talk like a decent human being."

The second one walks in quietly and heads toward the refrigerator. "I thought you were going out with the kids this afternoon," his mother calls.

"I decided not to. I'd rather watch TV."

"All you ever do is watch TV. Why don't you have friends like your brother?" She blocks the kitchen door. "There'll be no TV for you today. You can go out and play or sit on the front steps like a lump if you want."

The third one limps up the step, calling her mother. She has a bandage over her left eye.

"For heaven's sake, what happened?" her mother cries.

"Fell off my bike." She collapses on the sofa.

"Again?" her mother shouts. "That's twice this week. And last week you walked into a door."

"I can't help it. You could be a little sympathetic," the girl begins.

"Of course you can help it—be more careful." She walks away muttering, "Clumsy kid!"

The three parents in question—like millions of other parents throughout the country—have reacted with hostility.

"I'm supposed to congratulate her?" the first mother asks in defense. "A kid who's always mad and fighting I should feel good about?"

Margery looks mad. She acts mad. In truth, she certainly is mad—but not at her classmates, as her mother supposes. Margery is mad at herself. She sees her classmates enjoying each other: The girls share confidences; the boys flirt and kid around. They seem to belong together. Margery does not belong: No one flirts with her or pulls her aside to whisper a secret. She is different somehow and can't become one of the crowd, no matter how hard she tries to imitate them. So Margery is filled with hate—not for the insensitivity and vanity of those who reject her, but for her own ineptitude and lack of style.

However, if Margery admits even inwardly that she hates herself, she acknowledges failure. If, on the other hand, she turns her hostility around to direct it against her classmates, then she saves face—with herself.

Margery's mother never probes beneath the anger, and Margery's real feelings remain hidden, to fester and infect her whole personality.

The second mother is embarrassed. "What can you do with such a strange boy; he locks himself up in his room all day," she says.

With expectations derived from the gregarious Pepsi generation, this parent has stereotyped her son. He likes to be alone; he avoids basketball rallies and school dances; therefore, he is strange. If she scolds him adequately and forces him into the outside world, he will stop being strange, and then she will have peace of mind at last. Then people will not consider *her* strange for having raised such a son.

Actually, Peter is afraid. He is afraid that if he attends the class party, no one will talk to him; if he participates in the pep rally, he will have to sit alone. He finds it safer not to go find out. He knows he is safe in front of the television set or lying on his bed with the stereo blasting away. He sometimes wishes, ever so slightly, that he dared go to the party, but most of the time he doesn't even dare to wish.

His mother may not know for years. She accepts what she sees and hears from her own perspective. By the time the feelings erupt, it may be too late. Peter's personality will be unchangeable; his mother's chances of communicating with him, impossible.

The third mother is frustrated. "Wouldn't you be with the doctor's bills she hands us each month?"

A broken leg, a sprained ankle, cuts, bruises—Toni is always hurting herself. It seems her mother is continually receiving calls from school, not like phone calls other mothers receive to say their child is misbehaving—no, that would be easy. She gets phone calls to take Toni to the doctor or to meet the ambulance at the hospital. Such a clumsy kid! You would think she could be more careful.

Toni cannot be more careful. She is crying for help. She cannot understand why she feels so depressed or why she is so ugly or untalented. Her sister plays the violin; her brother is an A student. Margo, next door, is the most popular girl in the class. But Toni feels like nothing—nothing but clumsy.

Every time she has an accident, people fuss over her and worry and she knows they love her. She does not *purposely* have accidents, not so far as she knows. But Toni is accident-prone. And accident-prone is no accident.

Toni's mother has not tried to read her daughter's feelings and does not question the broken bones. She just scolds and calls her names. By the time she realizes that Toni is not just clumsy, Toni may have hurt more than a leg or an ankle. Teenage suicide is almost always a last cry for help—when all the other cries leading up to it have not been answered with understanding.

These parents love their children. They want to do their best for them, but they simply do not hear them. They are too busy judging. Judging stops up the ears of most parents.

Parents, and teachers too, begin judging in the earliest years. An infant who cries "with no reason" is labeled "spoiled." A preschooler who breaks a glass ashtray is called "careless." A child who gets Sunday school clothes muddy is considered "disobedient."

The process continues into school. In kindergarten, when a child throws a block, the teacher says it's "naughty." An obscenity carved into the desk is "dirty." Not studying is "irresponsible." Experiments with sex are "immoral." Driving 70 mph, he is being "reckless." Getting into alcohol or drugs is being "disturbed." Committing a crime is being "a bad kid."

In every case parents and teachers see only the behavior and react to that alone, with a label. They see the act. They do not see—nor do they try to see—the feeling behind it. They do what Margery's, Peter's, and Toni's parents did: They judge.

While judgment blocks hearing, it does not block response: punishment follows soon after. The schoolchild gets sent to the principal, has the parents called in, stays after school, is suspended. At home, television is taken away, the child is grounded, can't use the car, may even be institutionalized. Adults are quick to *do* something; they are slow to *hear*.

Yet in each action, from the smallest beginning in the crib, children such as this are trying to say something. They feel unhappy. They cry out for help. They are frightened or frustrated or lonely. They feel inadequate, isolated, confused. They do not know how to communicate these feelings, so they cry at first. No one hears. They scream, and still no one hears.

As they grow, the screams turn outward to acts of violence: hitting, breaking, vandalizing, stealing, assaulting. Or the screams turn inward to withdrawal: fantasies, daydreams, cutting class, getting drunk, dropping out of school, popping pills, roaming alone. The next step? Suicide.

Newspaper articles have shocked readers with the evidence of our youth's cries for help over the past decade.

Parents are horrified by the headlines, the articles, the statistics about teenage suicide and drug abuse and crime. And still they turn deaf ears to the cries of their own children.

"Why?" is the question. "Why do they do it?"

"Why?" one must echo. "Why do they fail to seek the answer at home?"

THE COMMUNICATION BARRIERS

There are three main blocks that keep parents from seeing the behavior of their children as the cry for help that it is.

Guilt

If parents discover what the poet Elizabeth Barrett Browning understood, that "the child's sob in the silence curses deeper than the strong man in his wrath," they will probably feel guilty. They will do to themselves what they do to their children: judge. And in their judgment, they will label themselves as "bad parents."

We still live with the myth of happy childhood. Parents who find the myth destroyed cannot accept the truth for what it is: simply a myth destroyed. They must brand themselves as the destroyers—not of the myth but of the childhood happiness itself. So completely have they bought the myth that they cannot even judge it; they can only judge themselves.

If parents respond to the misery within their child, they admit the misery and admit themselves as the cause of it. "What did we do wrong?" echoes under every headline of teenage tragedy. For in those cases, the truth has exploded in the parents' faces and cannot be avoided. Their child has cried so loudly that the whole world hears. Then parents, too, are forced to hear. And when they do, they know they have failed.

But until that last loud cry, parents resist hearing the communications of their child. If they hear it, they must blame themselves. If they do not hear it, they can blame society.

"Jane's school has no discipline," a father explains when his daughter is caught vandalizing.

"Steven wouldn't have stolen the car if his friends hadn't dragged him along," says a mother.

"If the police would clamp down, my kids couldn't get drugs," says another.

"How can you expect honesty from a kid when the whole world is so corrupt?" asks a father.

As long as they respond to their children's *behavior*, they are safe. They find explanations to get themselves off the hook. The parents mete out punishment that keeps them in control—for as long as possible. If they were to respond to their child's *feelings*, they would themselves feel too much pain, too much guilt, to bear. So they do not listen. They do not hear. They do not communicate. They do not know.

Threat

In the best sense of the word, experience is the process of awareness of what is happening inside us during a given situation—what we are feeling, what we are thinking, what we are doing. Learning is the direction we allow the experience to take us. It necessitates change.

Children spend their years in a whirl of learning, "changing from day to day," we say. They experience falling and walking, discovering, failing, wanting and getting and not getting. They learn about love and hate and atoms and foreign lands and sex and themselves. They are open to experience, and their minds are open to learning. They are unafraid to change.

As children turn into adults, however, they begin to believe what the world reiterates: that change is scary. For change entails giving up one thing with which you are secure for a new thing about which you are uncertain. You discard a known for an unknown. If you have always believed that war is a noble way to serve your country, you cannot safely risk throwing out that belief to sympathize with a pacifist. If you have always felt secure thinking that men are more capable than women, you would rather cling to that idea than switch and support the Women's Movement. And in both cases, because you are holding on to your beliefs so tightly, you will be threatened by the pacifist or the Women's Libber who passes your way.

So, afraid of change, you do not listen to what the Quakers or the members of NOW have to say. When opposing ideas enter the mind, the original beliefs could quaver and topple and have to be swept away. What will replace them is so unknown, so unsure and frightening, that it is better to keep opposing ideas out. The status quo is comfortable to live with.

Emerson knew what he was talking about when he said, "A foolish consistency is the hobgoblin of little minds."

Faced with the threat of changing ideas, many parents deafen themselves to their children's cries. During the late 60s and early 70s, parents were enraged by teenagers who grew scraggly beards and long hair, wore sandals and unironed shirts. Parents had in mind an image of how young people used to look and should look; it did not jibe with what they saw.

Part of what the young people were trying to say through their dress was simply, "We see you driven by materialism and that makes us angry. We want to love each other instead of money."

But their parents failed to hear the communication because they threw static in the way and jammed the lines. "Children should be clean and neat," they were saying as they turned their sons and daughters away. "They shouldn't smell bad." So instead of listening to their message, they drove their children through judgments and moralizing out of their lives to places visible, such as Haight-Ashbury and Greenwich Village, and places invisible, in the corners of their rooms and their minds.

Had they listened, the idea of a new value system would have met the one on which they built their lives. The fear of what might happen to their old values kept them deaf.

The diary of a college freshman was found after he hanged himself on a shower rod. He had written, "I love you, Mom and Dad, but I can't make you understand what I have to say."

Lack of Skill

If your daughter embarks on a living-together relationship, many messages—both spoken and silent—will be delivered.

Aloud, your daughter may say, "It's nothing. Everyone does it." But her real message could be, "I'm too afraid right now to make a further commitment."

Aloud you might say, "I forbid it. Don't bring him into *my* house." Actually, you may really want to say, "I love you, but I have been brought up to think this is immoral, and I don't know how to handle it."

Unfortunately, you and your daughter hear only the spoken messages, which drive each other in opposite directions.

No parent wants to sever communications with a child; no parent wants to alienate a child. Lack of communication skills make it happen.

LEARNING COMMUNICATION SKILLS

The answer, then, appears obvious: Learn the skills. How? What are they? Although communicating is a complex interchange, it can be divided into three main skills: looking, listening, and speaking. Let us examine each one separately.

Looking

Several years ago a book called *Body Language* by Julius Fast introduced the thought that people can understand each other through alertness to what their bodies are doing: how they stand and sit and walk, where they look, what they do with their hands. Unfortunately, instead of opening the lines of communication between people, body language turned into a parlor game, like palm reading.

Yet bodies do speak a language loud and clear. What we need is to learn to translate it. The best place to begin is by observing the physical: posture, muscle tension, eye expression, hands, sitting position, eye position, set of mouth, stance, lift of the chin, head position.

Your observations of these most basic signs may tell you more about your child than words do. You can see anger in the forward thrust of stance, in muscle tension, in a set jaw, in a rigid neck. You can see fear as the child pulls back from the world. One mother noticed that every time her son sat, he chose a chair in which he wrapped himself up like an embryo. Another realized that her daughter always looked away when they talked. Although these signs in themselves are of little significance, taken as part of the whole picture they speak to you.

While you're at it, you might check your own body language. What are your hands saying while you scold your child? One father found himself clenching his fists as if he wanted to punch his daughter. What are you saying as you lean back in your chair to listen? Perhaps that you are not very much interested. And your eyes, what are they saying? Are they stretched wide open to stare your child down, or are they relaxed and sharing?

As you learn to observe your child, begin looking beyond the physical. Look at your child's *health*. Any allergies? Do colds occur frequently? Accidents? What about upset stomachs and headaches? Any trouble with teeth? Dentists find tension quick to express itself in teeth and gums.

We know the close relationship between body and emotions. We accept ulcers and migraines as evidence of stress in adults. However, in our efforts to make our children behave, we forget to look for the same relationship in them. Let your child's health help you hear what he or she is saying. A medical checkup is not the stopping point; it is only the beginning of your attempt to understand.

Look at your child's *habits*. Is there trouble with sleeping? Is the child alone most of the time, or always with a crowd? How about sex: Is there avoidance? Overindulgence? Is schoolwork done? Does the child fly off the handle? Bite finger nails, pull hair, overeat, undereat? Is hair left uncombed? Does the child keep fairly clean?

Above all, are these habits changing? One does not worry

about a child who has always been messy the way one would about a neat child who has suddenly become messy or vice versa. Sudden changes of habit are an indication of problems within a child and should not be ignored.

"These kids are driving me crazy," a father complains. He sees their habits only as irritating behavior that he has tried to remedy. But nothing works—not the $100 he offers his daughter to stop biting her nails, not the threat of a cut in allowance if his son doesn't start working at school. Nagging does not communicate. Threatening does not communicate. It is time for another approach.

Try to look at the habit for what it is: a survival technique. Habits are formed by repeating behavior that works. If a girl is tense, perhaps chewing her fingernails offers temporary release; soon she is no longer aware of doing it. If a boy feels too "dumb" to do his homework, he goes to school with it undone. He hasn't tried; he cannot fail. He becomes the F student.

Elaine Barbour, the 1978 National Teacher of the Year, teaches with penetrating understanding. "There is no child," she says, "who would not rather look lazy than dumb."

Listening

"Don't tell me to listen to that girl," a mother complains. "What's to hear? She won't even answer me."

Other parents know the feeling. They too ask questions.

"What did you do in school today?"

"Same old thing."

"Where are you going?"

"Nowhere."

"How do you feel?"

"O.K."

It does seem as though your children tune you out of their lives, resenting your questions as intrusions. They are ungrateful, you claim, disrespectful too, and certainly uninterested in you. As usual, your mind goes into action, allowing you to see *them* as the cause of noncommunication.

Try to stop blaming and look at yourself. How do you try to get a conversation going with your child? What questions do you ask? Probably you ask *why*. And that is a sure conversation stopper.

When your child comes home from school screaming, "I'm so mad I could die," or falls into the front room in tears, your natural reaction is "why?" You want to know what happened.

But "why?" is a dead-end question. First of all, *your child probably does not know*. What answer do you expect?

"I'm angry because I didn't say anything when the kid across the aisle took my pen and didn't return it. I'm angry at myself for being so damned weak."

Or, "I'm crying because nobody chose me to be on their team in gym this afternoon. I'm crying because I'm sad about being so nonathletic."

Children are not capable of saying such things because they don't understand. If they did, they would be better able to handle the situation in the first place.

Second, *your child is intimidated by your question.* "Why?" is a demand. It bangs on the door of your child's private world like a policeman, insisting on entry. The tenderness within that world is afraid to let so forceful a visitor enter. It is safer to bolt the door with silence.

There are alternatives that enable you to draw your child out, giving the needed help and support. The following openers work far better:

"I know you're angry. Can you tell me anything about it?"

Or, "I can see that you're sad. You must feel just awful."

Or, "You're really upset, that's evident. Something must have happened in school today."

Openers like these do not threaten a child in the way a direct "Why?" does. They do not *demand*; instead, they *encourage* an explanation. Neither do they push for reasons that aren't understood. Instead they provide a choice as to whether to let you in or not. The child feels confident to cope with the question and feels secure in your gentleness.

Sometimes you need to go further in offering reassurance.

"I know that feeling," a parent may add. "It hurts."

Or, "Remember how angry I got last week? Is that something like the way you feel now?"

Or, "Crying helps me relieve my sadness sometimes. Does it yours?"

By sharing your own feelings and experience, you give still stronger support. Now when you are allowed into this private, hurting world, your child knows you enter with similar hurts. It is safer to share. It is easier to talk.

Hearing

Even with supportive questions and a child ready to share, parents often cut off communication. They listen, but they do not hear. They sit waiting to jump in with, "I think you should do this," or, "When I was your age, I . . ." Sometimes they do not even sit waiting; they interrupt.

If you have successfully opened a conversation, if your child has confidently allowed you to share these feelings, then *listen. Hear what is said.* Don't tolerate talk just so you can have your say in the end. Get involved in the feelings expressed, care about them, let them penetrate.

If you do not, your child will be a lot less willing to talk next time, and soon the lines of communication may be clamped off. Only the cursory "O.K." will be left, with you wondering, "Why doesn't my child ever talk to me?"

Understanding

George is about to take his SAT's. He is terrified.

"My whole future depends on this," he cries to his father. "What if I do badly?"

"You've got nothing to worry about. Forget it," his father answers. "Of course you'll do well. You always do."

George looks at his father for a moment in silence, then turns and goes into his bedroom. He cries most of the night—and not about the SAT's. He cries because his father has cut him off. He feels that his father just doesn't care about him.

Actually, George's father means well; he wants to cheer George up and give him confidence. Instead he does just the opposite.

First of all, *he denies George's feelings.* Instead of letting him know that he understands his son's worry, he tells him, as surely as though he had put it into words, "You shouldn't be worried. If you are, you're stupid. Exams don't matter."

But exams *do* matter to George, and he *is* worried, no matter what his father says. By denying rather than sharing his concern, his father pushes him inside and locks himself out. Both are left alone.

Second, *he puts an almost unbearable pressure on George.* George has to live up to his father's image of him. What George heard him say is, "I love you because you do well in school. Don't let me down on this exam." His father leaves him no room to do badly this time. He has to succeed—or else.

How could George's father have replied to his original expression of fear without cutting him off and without pressuring him? He could have said any number of things:

"I'm sure you feel now that your whole future depends on these SAT's, but it will seem less important later."

Or, "I can see how worried you are. Is there anything I can do to help?"

Or, "What if you do do badly? We'll take care of that one if it arises."

Any of these replies will give George the reassurance he is seeking and will keep his father a privileged visitor to his confidential world.

Talking

Janet has a problem. Her mother knows this from the way she has been acting lately—not eating or sleeping and moping around after school. She has finally been able to draw Janet out enough to find out what's going on.

"It's Greg," Janet says. "We've had sex."

Her mother gasps. "You've had what?"

Janet shifts in her chair. "Sex," she murmurs.

"Janet, I'm shocked," her mother begins. "I can't believe you would do such a thing. How could you?"

Janet begins to answer, then stops, sitting quietly while her mother finishes her tirade. She never brings up the subject again. Janet and her mother have fallen right into the so-called generation gap.

Janet's mother has severed communication lines by moralizing—a no-win method. While Janet seeks help, she gets only a lesson. She is confused over two value systems. She seeks help in decision-making and all she gets is the label of right and wrong.

What can her mother say instead of moralizing?

She can begin by saying, "Sex is a heavy matter. I can understand why you're upset."

Or, "I have been worried about you. Thank you for sharing with me."

Or, "Do you feel this is a problem between you and Greg or within yourself?"

Any of these nonthreatening openers is far more apt to elicit an honest conversation, leading into a discussion of responsibility and contraception in due course.

No matter how horrified her mother is, she cannot lecture her daughter into celibacy. All she can do by lecturing is drive her into lone decision-making that she will never share. That is sad for Janet and her mother; they need each other. That need unmet has filled many a psychiatrist's hour in later years.

Communicating

If you are not communicating with your child . . .

1. Make a sincere effort to look, listen, hear, and talk as discussed.

2. That failing, set up a parent-child meeting with the guidance counselor at school. Often an objective third party, especially one trained in human relations, can help break down barriers. Once the guidance counselor has enabled you and your child to listen to each other and to talk, you will be able to continue the process at home without needing a third person.

3. Work with your school Parents' Association to set up student-parent discussion groups. Some schools have done this as a one-shot assembly, where a panel of students and parents answers questions from the floor. Others have designated a day as student-parent day, kicking off with a speaker and then breaking into small discussion groups. Still others have organized seminars that meet regularly in an open exchange of ideas between parents and students. Specific topics are selected for each

seminar's discussion—such as sex, television, homework, politics, dating. An exchange of this kind cannot fail to extend the lines of communication into the home.

4. If you have tried everything and are still unable to communicate with your child, see a family counselor. A psychiatrist works on individual problems; a family counselor works with the group as a unit. When members are isolated from each other, the family system is breaking down. No single person, but rather the system itself, is the cause. Something is amiss with the dynamics. A family counselor pulls members together, helping them see where the system is failing and in what way alternatives can be found to put it back in working order.

Eleanor Roosevelt called understanding "a two-way street." You and your child must learn to walk in both directions in order to have that street bridge the gap between you.

Just as a radio requires a sender and a receiver, so communicating requires a listener and a speaker. When the listener is also the speaker and the speaker the listener, static fades away. The message of caring comes across so clearly that the space between the two diminishes to the closeness of a touch.

Dear Mrs. Miller:

My daughter, Elaine, reads too much. That may sound like a silly complaint, but it's true. She is thirteen years old and doesn't take part in school activities—she says she would rather stay home and read. Is that normal?

S. T.

Dear S. T.:

What is normal? Elaine can be different from her peers and still be perfectly normal. If she were watching television instead of reading, I would be worried—not for her normality, but for her mind. However, reading is an active pastime in which she exerts herself intellectually and emotionally. People grow and develop from reading, as well as from social activities. However, she may, as

you seem to feel, use reading as an escape from social
competition in which she feels insecure. Why not discuss
the possibility with her? Give her support. Make her feel
attractive. See whether she feels up to trying one or two
social events. She would be more comfortable going with
a classmate. Whatever you do, don't push . . . don't nag
. . . don't scold. Help her gain confidence . . . don't undermine it.

Dear Mrs. Miller:

I am a teacher in junior high school. Each year there are a
few girls who seem oversexed. They dress in tight, revealing
clothes, wear too much makeup, hang around the boys and all
over them. They look and act cheap. I am worried about what
will become of them. Can I do anything to help?

A Teacher Who Cares

Dear Teacher:

*Yes, I think you can do a lot. First, talk to the
girls—individually. Describe what you see, trying to give
them an objective look at their behavior. Let them know
that sexual interest is completely normal at their age,
but that there are other ways to act upon it. If that
doesn't work, have the guidance counselor or school psychologist speak with them. Often girls who feel unloved
at home—particularly by their fathers—overtly seek attention from other males. The school specialists may call
for a parent conference. You may not be able to solve the
problem immediately, but your caring concern may help
the girls over a rough period in their lives. And whatever
happens, they will be grateful that you didn't lecture
them and moralize.*

Dear Mrs. Miller:

I have been a widower for six years, raising two children—
a boy now fifteen and a girl thirteen. Things are going fine

with the boy, but my daughter has become rebellious and hostile, fighting everything I say or do or believe in. I feel like a total failure and don't know where to turn.

A Desperate Dad

Dear Dad:

Thirteen is a difficult age for girls even when they have two parents who feel as frustrated as you do. It is a time of contradiction: seeking independence, yet clinging to security; awakening sexual excitement, yet fearing unknown feelings; wanting to be beautiful, feeling ugly. The absence of a mother heightens the confusion and adds a feeling, however illogical, of rejection. Perhaps an aunt or a close woman friend could act as surrogate mother. Perhaps the school guidance counselor can be called in to help; he/she may suggest outside therapy for a while. Most important, however, is the support you give your daughter to make her feel loved. This feeling builds the self-confidence she needs to pass through these tumultuous years into adulthood.

Dear Mrs. Miller:

I have a fifteen-year-old sister, Mary. Each school year—from September through June—she unconsciously pulls out her eyelashes when under stress. Mom is frantic, and although Mary is unaware of *when* she is doing it, she knows she does it. I certainly would like to know what to do.

E. M.

Dear E. M.:

For some reason Mary feels extreme pressure to succeed—pulling her eyelashes is the release valve. With some it is nail-biting or hair twisting. Look for a solution as a whole family, trying to determine from where the pressure is coming. Is the work at school too difficult for her? Is she competing with you or with other siblings? Is she trying to live up to demands your parents set down? Is she afraid she won't be loved if she fails? Obviously, she is insecure about herself and looks on success as the

*way to status and acceptance. Talk to her teachers and
talk among yourselves—always including Mary. If the
problem continues, I suggest outside help—family therapy, perhaps.*

Dear Mrs. Miller:
    Our five-year-old began the year nicely. He trotted off to
kindergarten with a smile and seemed to love it. Suddenly he
has begun crying in the morning, saying he is afraid to go to
school. Nothing has changed at home—no baby, no divorce, no
deaths. What could have happened? What can we do?
J. Q.

Dear Mrs. Q.:
    *Fears develop easily in children. When they are ex-
pressed, as your son's are, parents and teachers are able
to guide them through the fears. It is when fears are held
inside or run away from or denied by parents that they
grow and become real problems. Try to get your child to
talk about his fear. Can he pinpoint it? What does he
think will happen in school? Or is he afraid of something
on the way to school? If it is a fantasy fear (a wolf in the
classroom, for instance) keep him talking about it. What
makes the wolf appear? What makes him go away? You
will certainly want to alert the teacher to this. If it is a
real fear (a teacher scolding or a child hitting him) make
an appointment for both of you to discuss it with the
teacher. Be alert to the frequent crossover of real and
imagined fears: a wolf in the classroom might easily be a
bigger child who frightens your son. The key to handling
children's fears is to take them—real or fantasy—seriously. Listen and support the child as he faces them and
works through them.*

Dear Mrs. Miller:
    In the sixth grade at our son Matthew's school, sports is
the big deal. The boys that are good athletes are the big shots.

The boys that aren't are looked down on and made fun of. Matthew is one of those who aren't. Can you advise me?

J. F. T.

Dear J. F. T.:

The best thing you can do is give Matthew constant support. Let him know that you consider him wonderful, sports or no sports. Share his hurt with him—discuss it, make him aware that you know what it feels like so he won't feel so alone in the world. In addition, help him find unique strengths of his own. Would he be interested in music or art lessons? Acting? Mime? Trips to the museum might get him involved in science, anthropology, oceanography. What about ham radio? The Y or Scouts or community environmental activities may offer him something. When he is a little older, he can do volunteer work with children or the aged. And interests like these can lead to involvement. He can become a specialist, and that—like sports—wins status in schools, too.

5/Discipline—for Better or Worse

A recent nationwide survey indicated that discipline is the chief educational concern of parents. "Get tougher on kids" was the overwhelming sentiment. The Rawsons are parents who agree— in theory, that is. In practice, they mean, "Get tougher on other people's kids."

Jack Rawson, an A student and president-elect of the student body for the coming year, handed in history and English papers that the teachers found were plagiarized. Confronted with the evidence, Jack admitted his guilt, and his parents were called in. Expressing disbelief, shock, disappointment, and anger in succession, they scolded their son, thanking the teachers for following through on the wrongdoing. "He has to learn," they said. Everyone was on the same side, and it looked as though Jack would emerge with a positive learning experience.

The principal, pointing out that had Jack plagiarized in college he would have been expelled instantly, talked with the teachers about disciplinary action. They wanted Jack to know the seriousness of plagiarism but also wanted to give him a second chance.

"We have decided to give him an F on both term papers," the principal explained.

"Can't you give him a chance to rewrite them?" his parents asked.

"And we are asking him to resign his student presidency next year."

"Resign?" his parents echoed.

"Yes," the principal explained. "We can't see his values serving as an example for other students."

Jack's parents rose in protest, grabbed their son by the arm, and stormed to a lawyer's office—to sue both the school and the principal for cruelty. Fortunately, no lawyer would take the case.

The Rawsons are one reason school discipline is ineffective. They, and many other parents, cry "too much leniency" until their own children are involved. Then they shout "injustice." What is discipline with others becomes heartlessness with theirs. Under such a double standard, effective discipline is doomed.

Actually, nobody is even sure what the word "discipline" means. Is it the *training* that develops controlled behavior? Or is it the *result* of the training—self-control itself? Or is it yet the mere *punishment* meted out in efforts to make the training work? Actually, it is all three. And that is too much of a definition for any word. It only adds to the confusion to realize that "discipline" comes from the same word as "disciple." What a harsh transition it has made through time!

APPROACHES TO DISCIPLINE

Instead of worrying about defining the word, which is contradictory at best, parents and teachers will gain more by determining what they want to accomplish through discipline. It is used for several ends.

Discipline as Punishment

When children are naughty, parents punish them. They may be spanked or sent to bed without dinner or deprived of a favorite television show. Punishment is as old and as acceptable as the Bible: "An eye for an eye, a tooth for a tooth."

Adults run into disciplinary punishment in their own lives. They have to pay fines for parking illegally; for more serious offenses, they are punished with jail or, in rare cases, with death. So when schools use discipline for the purpose of punishing a child, they act from a long line of historical examples.

Suspension is pure punishment, accomplishing little more than getting even with the child.

Humiliation is punishment—as it was in Colonial days when people were jeered at in the stocks or when scolds were dunked in water on the village green. Today the sarcastic tongue of a teacher in front of a class of peers is no less degrading or dampening to the spirit.

Spankings are punitive, although teachers have rationalized them as learning experiences under the guise of "Spare the rod, spoil the child." With as much vindictiveness as they used in the canings of olden days, teachers today still use physical punishment in forty-six of the fifty states in the nation. In fact, this nation, our United States, is one of only three countries in the entire world that have not yet outlawed physical punishment in schools—even though we forbid its use in the armed forces and in prisons.

Discipline as Correction

Discipline should serve as a corrective measure, but the usual kind meted out hasn't a chance because it is too contradictory. "Don't scream at me," screams a parent, or, "If you get into one more fight, I'll belt you." Our attempts at correction tend to confuse children.

Similar contradictions happen in school. A girl caught chewing gum, which was against school rules, had to stay after school and chew ten packs of gum in front of the teacher. A boy who did not turn in one page of homework was given twelve similar pages to do. A high school student who failed geometry was sent to summer school with the same teacher and failed again. Neither parents nor teachers seemed to use common sense in their discipline.

Do corrective measures in our own lives work any better? Does the speeding ticket make us drive more slowly or the Internal Revenue audit restrain us from cheating on income tax returns? When a police officer arrests a prostitute, does this teach her not to solicit? Does jailing teach the pusher not to sell dope?

Corrective discipline purports to be humane. But a New England principal struck and seriously injured a twelve-year-old when he tried to teach him a lesson for striking a classmate. In one extreme case, three Southern boys caught smoking cigarettes had to be hospitalized after they were corrected from committed future crimes by being made to chew up and swallow the cigarettes they had left. There must be better lessons.

Discipline as Authority

"Why do I have to apologize?" a child asks. "Because I say so," answers the parent.

This is the discipline of authoritarianism. The army is based on it—"A good soldier doesn't think; he obeys." The fascist state is built on it, as Hitler evidenced. And Solzhenitsyn's *Gulag Archipelago* shows that the Communist state is built on it as well.

Children live in an authoritarian world. Being unable to vote, they have no say about the laws of their country or of their community. As secondary citizens in the school system, despite token student councils, they have little say in matters most vital to them—curriculum, teaching methods, teachers. Even at home, their voices sound only in whispers or whines compared to those of their fathers and mothers.

Therefore, discipline to them is an assertion of authority— always someone else's. They have to be in school on time, they can't cut gym, they have to eat at twelve fifteen, they can't talk in the halls, they have to secure a permission slip to go to the toilet—all because *they* say so. *They* is the big nebulous power that disciplines their lives, seemingly without logic, without reason, and without a care as to what the students think.

If parents and teachers will imagine themselves in a similar situation of helplessness—like Alice in Wonderland—they will better understand the frustration that leads young people to lash out in the destructive ways they often do.

Discipline as Convenience

Most rules are laid down, both at home and at school, as a convenience for the powers that be rather than for the good of the children. When we say we want our son home by 9 P.M., it is often not because he might be hurt if he came in at 10 but because we want peace of mind an hour earlier. When schools insist on quiet in the halls, they avoid the inconvenience of teachers' having to speak above noise and having to compete with it; children, we know, don't even hear it. It is a moot point whether neat rows at home and in school lead to organized study habits; but it is certain that they cut down on work for mother and teacher, and so rules of neatness are established.

This is all right. We should be able to set up rules that make living with children as comfortable as possible. What we should not do is pretend that the rules are for the children's good. That is when we run into trouble, because children can argue us out of the rules with instant logic. And then we're in trouble because we have locked ourselves into the rules and can't back out.

"Just close my door, Mom," a son offers, "if you don't like the mess." He makes sense, but Mom can't do it; she usually insists on neatness on the grounds that it is better for him, not her. Not looking at his room does not change the situation for him (or even for her, since she *knows* what it looks like on the other side of the door), so the rule sticks. But she could have been honest in the first place and said, "Look, your messy room drives me crazy. Please clean it up." Then his suggestion of closing the door would have made sense, and a scene would have been avoided. Making the clean-up rule on the pretense of helping him virtually ensures a confrontation between them.

Even when children do not agree, if the rules are explained as a necessity for their parents' ease and sanity, they can be understood and accepted. Young people do respect honesty—and understand convenience.

JUVENILE INSTITUTIONS—THE ULTIMATE DISCIPLINE

The juvenile justice system in America is like the ultimate school. Children who have not learned citizenship anywhere else end up there. Multiple uses of discipline are in effect in juvenile institutions, which, because they form a closed world, can serve as a microcosm for study. An exploration of these institutions is likely to lead to a questioning of our own uses of discipline at home and to reevaluation of their success.

Punishment has put young people in the institution in the first place. They have hurt society; now society will hurt them back. They will suffer confinement, loss of family, humiliation, and boredom. After a designated period of punishment, they will be released back into society. Cured? Hardly. Punished? Yes.

Punishment, rather than curing, builds hostility and alienation enough to set a young person on a path of crime for life. While a youth usually enters an institution a minor criminal or no criminal at all—a runaway, a truant, a delinquent—he or she often exits with all the hostility of a real criminal.

When a child is angry enough to lash out against society, punishment only serves to heighten the anger. A recent study shows that corporal punishment in schools increases vandalism, the crime that brings a majority of young people to be corporally punished in the first place. And juvenile institutions prove that the dehumanizing effects of punishment make the crime problem worse. Citizens crying for harsher treatment of juvenile offenders—for example, New Yorkers whose legislature voted to send thirteen-year-olds into Criminal Court—are not solving the problems of street crime. They are intensifying it through harsher methods.

It seems clear that punishment—whether in juvenile institutions or in schools or at home—does not work. It does not lessen the original problem that elicited punishment but succeeds only in making the child angrier and more frustrated. The adults administering the punishment feel that they have not let the problem go but have "gotten even" with the child. It is not a constructive choice for either party.

Correction, or rehabilitation, was the going word in the juvenile justice system for years. Guidance help, encounter groups, corrective programs were installed to teach inmates better behavior patterns. Schools and work-release plans were added to help them acquire skills and to give them incentive for improvement. Indeterminate sentencing was tried to give them a chance to show how "good" they were becoming. Corrective discipline, it seemed, could not fail—yet recidivism rates remained high.

Young people appeared to be learning *inside* the institution, but once *outside* they reverted to their old ways and landed back in again. What was wrong? Was rehabilitation impossible? It appeared so.

What seems to have been happening was that young people were not being rehabilitated; they were playing the game. Authorities wanted them to smile, so they smiled. They wanted the kids to enjoy work, so they enjoyed work. They wanted them to show interest in school, so they did. They performed just as the authorities wanted them to, and they were released. Then they ran into the same old problems of poverty and joblessness and found themselves reverting to the old life-style. They did what they always had, which was *not* to smile and *not* to work and *not* to like school—until they got in trouble and landed back in the institution.

There are several important lessons to be learned here: *Corrective discipline cannot work in a punitive environment. Nor can it work under authoritarianism.* Nor can it work until basic socioeconomic problems are solved. Corrective discipline can work only in an atmosphere of trust when young people themselves are involved in it—as we shall discuss later on.

Authority is established in a hundred ways within a juvenile institution. This is no casual happening, but rather a deliberate design to dehumanize and subjugate. Uniforms, regimentation, locked doors, hours meticulously kept, glass doors through which kids are observed, room checks, body counts— these are only the obvious signs of an authoritarian world within the institution walls.

Correctional officers (one no longer calls them guards) are large and many and ever-present. Comradery draws them together. Hostility and mistrust keep the young people apart. So there is isolation and the them-against-me attitude of enemy camps.

Authority reaches down into the most personal aspects of life, especially sex. Institutions are unisex, and there is much teasing about deprivation, much boasting about prowess. Homosexuality is severely punished. Masturbation is barely dared in cells with three or more, and nearly impossible behind glass windows watched carefully by guards. Maybe once or twice a year girls and boys are brought together for a dance; sexuality vibrates, as the officers watch and laugh. They are the Authority. But young people are sexually hungry and clever and determined; even Authority can be outwitted.

Mere authority cannot work—not in a juvenile institution, not in school, not in home. As someone said, "You have not changed a man because you have silenced him." Authority merely silences—for a while.

A look at juvenile institutions testifies to the fact that all disciplinary rules are made for the *Convenience* of the institution, not of the inmates. Waking and sleeping hours are determined around staff hours; eating hours suit the kitchen crew. Jobs assigned to young people are not those that could help them develop but those that need doing—rocks to move, toilets to clean, dishes to wash. Locked doors at night reduce the need for officers to a minimum; available television sets help maintain quiet. Visiting days limit turmoil to one specific time. And so on—all in the name of helping young people in trouble.

Young people sit around complaining as they comply with all the rules. What else can they do, when these rules make no sense to them, humiliate them, and dehumanize them? Will there be an authority figure someday in an institution who will at least be honest with the inmates? Will there be someone who will someday say to them, "Look, we make these rules because we have to live too"? The inmates wouldn't particularly like what was said, but they would understand. And they might even grumble a little less next time they were assigned to cleaning the toilets; at least, they would know that Authority can be honest.

None of these disciplinary approaches works in juvenile institutions. If angry glowers and hostile words and escape attempts are not adequate proof of this, statistics are. Juveniles who have been institutionalized return at the rate of 80 to 90 percent. Discipline as punishment, correction, authority, or convenience is not overcoming socioeconomic factors and turning troubled youths into better citizens. Something else is needed.

Schools are not so different from juvenile institutions. Both have a built-in captive audience. Both are autocratic. Both set up a system of game-playing by which success is won. Both create a sense of failure within young people. Both fail to accomplish their stated goals: Juvenile institutions fail to minimize juvenile crime; schools fail to maximize learning. Both fall short of community and human needs.

In both cases, disciplinary measures—whichever of the four kinds has been used—do not work. Is there a fifth kind of discipline? An alternative?

CREATIVE DISCIPLINE

There is, of course—an approach I would call creative discipline. A few juvenile institutions and a few schools are trying it. Wise parents have used it for years without calling it anything. It works.

Creative discipline is as varied as the creativity of the people involved in it. There are no limits. You will understand it and be able to use it more constructively when you know the fundamentals from which it evolves.

Involving Young People in the Process

As discussed earlier, the disciplinary measures now being used generally fail because they are superimposed on young people, who react with hostility and a sense of failure. Creative discipline brings young people into the picture. It asks them, in effect, "What do you think should be done?"

Children have a great sense of justice. They know when they have done something wrong, and they know—usually better than adults—how to compensate. Understanding this, adults can use the strengths with which young people are equipped—both to help young people learn and to help themselves run smooth operations.

In the Courtroom

The juvenile justice system is experimenting with creative discipline with astounding results. A judge, for example, asks a youth who has broken into and robbed a store how he thinks amends should be made.

"Would going to Boys' Home do it?" the judge asks.

The young man shakes his head, eyes on the ground.

"What, then?" the judge persists.

The boy shuffles. "Pay the guy back?"

"That's a start. But what about the broken window? And what about his lost business?"

"I haven't got any more money than what I took, and I already spent some of that," the boy mumbles.

"Then how can you pay this man back for what you did?"

The boy looks up. "I could work for him." He pauses. "Couldn't I? If he let me?"

"I don't know," the judge answers. "Ask him."

The boy and the store owner come to terms on how many days the boy will have to work in order to pay back the stolen money and the damage. The sentence is passed. The case dismissed. The boy does not steal again.

Perhaps there are other, less successful scenarios. Maybe the store owner is afraid to take the boy into his store; maybe the boy, working for him, does steal again. But if creative discipline works only half the time—even if it works in only 20 or 30 percent of cases—the effort is well spent. Prison, an alternative, works less than 5 percent of the time.

In the School

Schools, in greater numbers than family courts, are effectively involving young people in their own disciplinary action. Some have an elected student Judicial Board that handles infractions of school rules. But while good in theory, in practice the board is apt to become as authoritarian as the school administration. It becomes an arm of the administration, doing the "dirty work" so that administrators remain innocent and lovable.

However, student disciplinary boards can operate in an open environment with great success. For instance, in a Michigan school the student board overruled the principal on a disciplinary measure concerning students who smoked marijuana. Instead of expelling them, as the principal had ordered, the student board suspended them for a week, and required them to compile findings on the effects of marijuana during that time.

Student involvement works with younger children too. In a Colorado community, for instance, an elected board of six students from grades four, five, and six handle discipline problems in one elementary school. A bus driver brought Greg before the board for daily misbehavior on the way to school. The children questioned Greg, who admitted that he poked children and jumped on his seat and yelled.

"Why do you act like this?" the board chairperson, a sixth-grade girl , asked.

"I dunno."

"But you *do* it," she persisted.

"Yeah." Greg searched for an answer. "I guess I want the kids to laugh at me."

"Is that the only way you can get them to laugh?" asked another board member.

"I know another way," a fourth-grade member injected.

"Let Greg figure it out," the chairperson said.

"I could tell a joke."

"Then from now on," she told him, "you tell jokes on the bus. O.K.?"

Greg nodded and left the room. After he had gone, the chairperson told her fellow board members, "Greg's mother has a new baby, and I think Greg feels left out."

"Let's get everyone to be real nice to him so he'll feel good," a fifth-grader suggested. "Then maybe he'll act nicer."

They did, and Greg did. And no adults in the world could have understood or handled Greg's problem with the effectiveness of that group of children.

At Home

Parents can involve their children in creative dicipline at home just as effectively. The Masons did.

Joe did poorly at school; his older sister, Beverly, did well. The parents nagged and scolded Joe, while Beverly used her power position to tease him. When Joe brought home report cards with straight D's and F's, his parents punished him by grounding him on weekends and cutting off television. When Beverly teased him about it, they sent her crying to her room. Home had become a nightmare.

"I feel like moving to the office," Mr. Mason confessed.

Then they decided to try a new approach. Gathering the

family together, Mr. Mason asked, "How do you feel about the way things have been going around here?"

All admitted they felt awful.

"Things used to be great until dummy Joe messed up in school," yelled Beverly.

"Yeah?" Joe defied her. "Things would still be great if you kept your smart mouth closed."

"You've got the trouble right there," said the mother. "You two can't stop fighting."

"I think," said the father, "we've got the trouble with *all* of us. We nag and punish. They pick and fight. There's got to be another way."

For the Masons, there is—now.

Joe and Beverly made their parents see that they put too much emphasis on school marks. So they eased up. Joe agreed to work harder if his parents would not nag. Beverly agreed to stop teasing and see whether she could help Joe with his work.

Together they decided to keep a chart. At the end of every week, they now see how many fights the family has had over school. If none, they treat themselves to a weekend movie. But if there have been fights, they call a family gathering to investigate what triggered them and how they could have been avoided.

Joe is not getting straight A's, and Beverly does not give up her favorite television shows to help him with math every night. Creative discipline does not work miracles. But Joe's report cards are filling up with C's, and he had a B minus last term in science. The Masons do not jump for joy over Joe's marks, but they do hug him and say, "Looks a lot better than it used to, doesn't it?" And Mr. Mason is once again glad to come home from the office at night.

Requiring a Positive Relationship

The director of Goshen Center for Boys in New York State was asked, "How do you keep boys from escaping?"

"There is only one way," he explained, pointing out the fallibility of doors and locks and gates. "That is in the relationship a boy develops with one of us."

Young people are more conscious of the value of a positive adult-child relationship than the adults in their lives are. When asked what they consider a good teacher, they are likely to reply, "One who cares." When asked what quality they most admire in their mother, they often answer, "She is a caring person." Caring is the basis of a good relationship. A student who feels that an adult *cares* not only admires and likes but also wants to please that adult—whether it is to pass math or not to escape from Goshen Center for Boys.

Caring is what makes most children want to please their parents. They care, and they know their parents care. So they adopt their parents' values and behavior and life-styles. It matters that they make them happy.

But when children feel that their parents do not care, there is no desire to please them. They reject their values; they rebel against their behavior; they seek alternative life-styles. Without caring, there can be no relationship.

And without a relationship, there can be no creative discipline. For with caring gone, young people see rules and regulations as no more than adult enforcements on their freedom. They see disciplinary measures as vengeance. "They hate us for being young," they say. "They envy us for being free."

Even caring adults, parents and teachers, often give the impression of coldness. They hide their caring under nags and threats; they hide the pleasure of their relationship under signs of disappointment. They hide these feelings well—so well that young people begin to feel they are loved only when they are "good," as adults define the word "good." When they are being themselves, that love hardens over with anger and punishment.

Yet there is no single quality more essential to constructive discipline than the feelings between the child and the adult involved. As a guidance counselor put it, "When there is a good relationship, almost no kind of discipline can be wrong. When there is a bad relationship, no kind can be right."

Seeking the Cause of a Child's Misbehavior

If communities used creative discipline, juvenile crime statistics might be cut in half. Most street crime is committed to get money—whether for cocaine or cars. Juveniles are caught, arrested, sent to institutions, and let back out after serving their time. However, nothing has changed; they still need money. And they still mug for the dollars in an old lady's purse. Their prison sentence does nothing about the cause of the crime: does not attempt to alleviate it, does not even acknowledge its validity.

Statistics show an alarming ratio between low reading and high crime. One of the things this may be telling us is that young people who can't read can't get jobs and, therefore, resort to stealing as a means of getting money. Yet the institutions to which they are sent can do very little to help them. They have schools, yes—perfunctory ones, usually far worse than the ones the juveniles dropped out of on the outside. The cycle is perpetuated. The community does not spend money to provide good education within the juvenile system in order to cut the crime rate. It just hires more policemen. The cause of juvenile crime is ignored.

Schools act in the same illogical way. If children do not work, the teacher assumes they are lazy and punishes them—by scolding or giving extra assignments or keeping them after school. As a result, they get angry and work even less, therefore receiving stronger punishment next time. And so on in the cycle.

Actually, these students are very probably not lazy; it is not in the nature of children to be lazy. Watch them work at something they want to do to find proof of this. It may be that these children are *bored* but that the teacher does not try to make the work more interesting for them. Perhaps they are *insecure,* but the teacher does not attempt to build their self-confidence. They may be *less able* than other students, but the teacher does not prepare special, less challenging work. In all cases, the teacher just keeps on giving the same work in the same way, only more of it, and punishing those children who don't do it—and the disciplinary measures are ineffective without an understanding of the students' behavior.

Parents, too, are quick to respond to their children's actions but slow to probe into the reasons for them. Yet until these reasons are uncovered, investigated, and removed, the behavior is likely to repeat itself.

Children are naturally curious, alert, eager to learn, responsive, loving. That is how they come into the world. That is how they learn to survive and grow. When their behavior changes, the cause must be explored. A wise parent asks "Why?" Sometimes the seriousness of a situation forces the question.

Jodi was a "wild" teenager; her brother Tim was quiet. Not until Jodi got in trouble drinking, and the family went into group therapy, was the reason for Jodi's behavior understood. Since childhood, she had felt that the only way to compete with her bright "good" brother was to be the exact opposite. Despite punishments in school and at home, she had persisted in her wild behavior. No one had looked beneath it. Even as a teenager, though, she was not too old to be helped once the cause was known; she found more constructive ways to compete—mainly through sports, at which she excelled.

When parents look beneath their child's behavior, they are forced to face a truth, often frightening and painful—that they themselves are a part of both the cause and the result. Families work together like a machine. No one part operates as a totally separate unit; the cogs fit together and turn each other. What each member does affects the whole family. Labeling family members as good or bad does not change its operation. Becoming aware and shifting positions can.

Creative discipline arises from working together for increased sensitivity and awareness and, most important, for change.

Knowing When Not to Discipline

There are times when no discipline is called for.

When a child has tried and failed, discipline will destroy. Try to be sensitive to the honest efforts of your children—not the panicky cramming for an exam but the year-long striving to learn. Share with your children the pain of failure—not always expressed in tears, more often in a laugh and a shrug. And accept, love, and be proud of your children, despite your own hurt pride.

When a child has paid in hurt, discipline has already taken place. If a child has hurled unrecallable words of anger at a friend or a parent, or has cried in front of the class after being scolded by the teacher, or has quit the basketball team in a rage—in all such instances, the child has already been punished. The parent should neither rush to protect nor add discipline, but instead should leave the child alone—to feel and work through the hurt and to emerge stronger and wiser.

When a child has erred from ignorance, discipline is superfluous. Did Grace yell "Shit" at the teacher because she heard it at home and did not consider it wrong? Did she copy a poem and turn it in as hers because she liked it and had no idea that this was an act of plagiarism? Did she fool around with sex because it was fun and she had not been taught to think about the consequences? In cases like these, parents should avoid the easy error of viewing the children's mistakes through their own painfully acquired knowledge and instead should view them through their children's true innocence. "Ignorance of the law is no excuse" may apply before a judge, but not necessarily before a parent. When a child does not *know* what he or she has done, the parent's job is to explain, not to discipline. The likelihood of repetition will be far less.

Bypassing discipline need not appear as a sign of weakness. Being too lazy to follow through is weak. But forgiveness is positive and strong. It acknowledges error as human, communicating what is even more important: love.

GUIDELINES FOR DISCIPLINE

Here are some general dos and don'ts of discipline for your consideration. If you keep them in mind, you may be able to deal with specific problems with greater confidence.

The Don'ts

Don't threaten a child and not follow through. If you have said, "You can't watch television if you are late for school today," stick to it. Don't back off when your child nags or cries or gives you a rough time. Show that you mean what you say. Once you let your child manipulate you out of carrying out a threat (which you probably shouldn't have made in the first place), your words mean nothing. You can be smart by following through on this threat—and make it easier for yourself by not issuing future ones.

Don't make a child apologize who does not feel sorry. A child who spoke back to the teacher may be sorry to have gotten in trouble but is probably glad to have spoken out. By insisting on an apology, you force the child to be a hypocrite. It may save face for you, but it teaches a destructive lesson: Pretending is better than being honest.

Don't punish a child for communicating what he or she has done. If you punish your child for admitting a lie, next time the child may stick to the lie. The lesson learned is that the truth does not pay. A child who confesses wrongdoing trusts you to understand and help. If you punish instead, you belie that trust, which you may never be able to rebuild again.

Don't create situations that invite misbehavior. Here are some examples:

Making an issue of only "bad" things your child does. Focus on "good" things too. Tell your child how you feel about them. Tell the teacher too.

Nagging. Children become deaf to nagging—the only way to survive it. Either make an issue of something that bothers you or forget it. Nagging is a sickly compromise between the two.

Denying your child love. No matter what a child has done, do not say, "I don't love you any more." And don't threaten by saying "If you do that, Mommie and Daddy will not love you." Loving comes with the job. Make sure your child is confident of that always.

Comparing one child to another. If one child behaves in school and one does not, comparing them only serves to make the disparity greater. Remember that each child is a separate entity and should be accepted as such—in strengths as well as in weaknesses.

The Do's

Set rules that can be kept. Whether they concern bedtime hours or school behavior, make certain that your child can keep those rules—and that you can enforce them.

Explain rules clearly. Honest misunderstandings cause many broken rules, and so do loopholes. Eliminate the possibility of both by explaining clearly and carefully what you expect.

Follow through on disciplinary action when rules are broken. Doing nothing about broken rules undermines both the rules and your role as a parent. Following through can frequently be an inconvenience and a downright pain to parents—it may mean giving up a weekend or a trip. But if you are not willing to follow through on a broken rule, do not make the rule in the first place.

Praise your child as well as punish, but don't overdo it. In praising a child, be aware that children recognize undeserved praise. They know when a picture they drew is careless and messy, so if you tell them it is wonderful, they will tend to disbelieve any praise you give them in the future. If you praise children too much, even when praise is deserved, you put them under pressure. They begin to feel that unless they continue to earn your praise, you will not love them, and the stress of having to succeed sets in. Therefore, praise—and punish—in moderation.

Make disciplinary action quick and reasonable. The old phrase "Wait until your father comes home" is ineffective. The child suffers all day in anticipation of Father's return home. By the time he arrives, whatever he does is pale in comparison to the day's torture. Mete out discipline immediately and let it be over with quickly. Then forget it. Do not harp on it every time you get angry at the child again.

Involve your children in setting down rules. When you involve your children, rules are understandable and more likely to be kept. You may be surprised to learn that your children have better ideas than you when it comes to making rules. Give them a chance to show you.

Involve your children in disciplinary measures. When they make mistakes, involve your children in deciding what to do. When you make mistakes, involve them as well. If you run on a double standard in which rules apply to them but not to you, you are operating an authoritative household. It doesn't work. It may maintain quiet, but it does not build a strong family.

Dear Mrs. Miller:
We used to be a happy, loving family. No more. My son and my husband are at each other all the time, fighting and nagging, screaming and yelling. I think they hate each other. Is there a solution?

Mrs. D. Q. A.

Dear Mrs. A.:
I have addressed your problem several times. Let me quote the wise words of a Maine Ladies' Home Journal *reader: "Children are not baby chickens or horses. Conflict between father and son is a necessary part of becoming mature. A father cannot silently let his son do things of which he disapproves. A boy must learn that adults live by their values and do not toss them aside for a while. On the other hand, a father must learn that a boy is an individual and will do some things a father would not."*
It is a fine line ... which may not console you. However, it is a line most families walk ... which may.

Dear Mrs. Miller:
How do you stop children from using bad words? We never use them ourselves, my husband and I, but our fifth- and seventh-graders bring them home from school and use them constantly. It is embarrassing.

Mary W.

Dear Mary W.:
First of all, stop being embarrassed—your friends and neighbors have heard those words before, if that's what is upsetting you. You have heard them before too. They are only words. Why do the children use them? Because they think it is grown up? Because they want to shock you? Because they want to assert their own values? Discuss the subject with them and find out. Whatever

*their reason is, perhaps you and they can come up with
alternatives that will be both more acceptable and more
effective.*

Dear Mrs. Miller:
    My husband and I cannot agree on ways to discipline our
children. He says we have to be tough; I say we have to be
more gentle. It's gotten to the point where we cause more
problems in deciding how to discipline the kids than they do
in misbehaving. What's the answer?

                                                        L. T.

Dear L. T.:
    *The answer for you and your husband is to figure
out what your basic differences are. Do you agree on the
seriousness of your children's misbehavior? Do you agree
on what you hope the discipline will accomplish? Do you
agree on your roles as parents and how you should relate
to your children? Until you come to an understanding on
these issues, you cannot come to one on discipline. If you
can't reach an agreement on anything, I think you
should consult a guidance counselor or a family therapist. Continuing to pull the children in opposite directions, as you now are, can only harm them.*

Dear Mrs. Miller:
    What are your thoughts on spanking children? Are there
times when it is right?

                                            Mr. and Mrs. S.

Dear Mr. and Mrs. S.:
    *In a word, NO. There are times when a parent would
like to hit a child, but I do not think there are times
when it produces constructive results. Spanking tells a
child that violence is acceptable. It also shows that the
parents are up against a wall and do not know what else*

to do. Be creative. You can come up with more effective
means of discipline.

Dear Mrs. Miller:
Every once in a while I get really angry at my children
and I yell at them. My husband says my temper is damaging
to them. Is he right?

A. L.

Dear A. L.:

*An adult temper tantrum (if that is what you have)
tells children that they can make their parents lose control. That's not good, and it can be frightening to your
children to know they have such power. But if, soon after
the blowup, you talk about your anger with them, I don't
feel it has been damaging. Your anger tells your children
that other people besides them feel mad sometimes. They
learn that it is a normal feeling—and that can be reas-
suring.*

*Anger can be handled more effectively than by yell-
ing, however. I know a mother who says, "I am so angry
that I do not want to be near you," and goes to her room.
Her children repent far more quickly than if she had
spanked them.*

6/Handling School Problems

Children have always gotten into trouble in school. They have been sassy and fought and lied and copied tests and invented excuses for undone homework. Teachers have washed their mouths out with soap, stood them in the corner, caned them, and made them wear dunce caps. Still, they continue to get into trouble.

Today, trouble has taken on more frightening aspects. More than 70,000 teachers are injured by students each year—seriously enough to require medical attention. This is no longer mere talking back.

Since 1970, assaults on students by other students have risen 85 percent across the nation. Tom Sawyer is no longer fighting only with his fists.

In some urban areas, as many as 90 percent of students are not reading on grade level. This goes beyond a bad report card.

Over half a million teenagers are drinking to excess. At least 30 percent of the nation's teenagers are experimenting with drugs and turning on countless numbers of elementary school children along with them. The old crime of smoking on the school fire escape looks tame in comparison.

Every day two and a half million enrolled students are absent from school. An additional two million eligibles are not even enrolled. The truant officer can no longer handle the job.

Fifty percent of all students admit to cheating "occasionally." Honor codes are being abolished.

Stealing is rampant. Teachers have to lock up their purses; students, their personal belongings. The days of the cubbyhole storage area are gone.

Times and crimes have grown more threatening. Parents need greater wisdom than ever before—not just to avoid problems but to handle them. In their bafflement they seek understanding; in their helplessness, a way to help. Until they face themselves, however, they can find neither. Nor are young people really facing up to their problems. They feel it is the schools' fault, their parents' fault, society's fault; they are victims.

In their joint efforts to evade responsibility, parents and children (and their teachers, alas!) avoid facing not only the problem but—inevitably—the solution. Until they are willing to admit to the problem, examine it, and assume responsibility for solving it, there is no hope; children will act out and parents and teachers will not see. Even the bold typeface of horror headlines will not alert them to potential danger until the names of their own children are emblazoned.

Confronting problems hurts. Parents lose face; young people may lose some freedom. But there is no other way. The nagging, scolding, threatening, and punishing that parents and teachers have done for years have not solved problems; they have only afforded temporary escape from the main issue. The rebelling, copping out, and running away of young people have been similarly unsuccessful. Problems must be met head-on: Band-Aid treatment does not work.

School programs generally can be seen as falling into four main categories: academic, behavioral, social, and moral. In this chapter I will explore each of these areas in turn and offer guidelines for their handling.

ACADEMIC PROBLEMS

Four parents open their children's report cards.

Edna has worked hard all year. She has worried even harder. A petite, pretty tenth-grader, she wears a perpetual frown. She rarely smiles, and she shrinks when anyone looks at her. She accepts the fact that she is not as smart as her older brother, Al, who is going to Colgate next year. And she is resigned to her father's scornful "Dumb" when he reads her report card.

He is reading it now, a report card that looks like a Xerox copy of last term's: *Math—F:* "If Edna would make herself learn theorems, she would do better in geometry." *History—D:* "Edna must work harder to retain the material she covers." *English—D—:* "Edna's English mark will improve when she learns to handle abstract ideas." *French—F:* "Edna does not know her verbs."

"Are you proud of this?" her father asks.

Edna looks down.

"What do you do to get such marks?" he continues. "You know what you do? Nothing. You do nothing—just sit around dumb all day."

Edna still looks down. She used to cry when her father talked to her. Now she just looks down.

The truth is that Edna does not do "nothing" all day. She works hard in school. She spends her free time in the library and starts her homework the minute she gets home. But she does not understand the lessons in the first place and cannot remember the teachers' explanations.

So her homework is returned with an F. Edna sometimes talks to her teachers, who explain again and tell her to "keep trying." But they know that Edna will not understand any better this time. At report card time she gets her D's and F's and takes makeup exams and goes home and her father calls her dumb. The same thing happens next semester and next year—as if she were adding link after link to a chain.

No one breaks the chain by taking a real look at Edna's problem.

Bob does not work—not at his lessons; he works at ways to avoid them. He loses assignment pads or forgets his books or breaks his eyeglasses. He works at inventing excuses to fool his teachers and his parents too.

Bob's parents know that this big, heavy boy of theirs is a clown. They thought he was cute in elementary school with his jokes on the teacher and his ingenuity in evading responsibility. They still think he is cute now that he is in high school.

"That kid of ours is a riot," they say. "He got the teacher to raise his mark by convincing him he had forgotten to give a certain lesson."

They have fun when Bob joins them for television after dinner.

"Don't bullshit me, boy," his father laughs. "You haven't done your homework." Bob pantomimes shock.

His mother laughs. "He'll do it later."

Today when Bob's parents open his report card, they find a C, two C—'s, and two D's.

"Bad, huh?" Bob asks, pretending to burst into tears.

"You better work next semester," his father says. "Work twice as hard to make up for that goofy Miss Nutham or Nuthead or whatever her name is."

Bob will not work next semester—or the one after that. He will never work because he does not know how and has no need to learn. His parents have programmed him for "success" without working. He is a con man, a wheeler-dealer, an operator. He gets along by fooling his teachers, his parents, and, above all, himself.

His teachers do not understand. They type routine comments on his report card that make sense only in the context of their own world: "Bob has to work harder," "When Bob settles down to work, he will do well," or, "Bob is bright enough to know he has to work harder."

But they are wrong, because Bob does not have to work harder. He is doing just fine the way he is. He is passing school, his parents adore him, and he feels good about ripping off the world.

If only one person cared enough to refuse the rip-off, Bob could be helped.

Bruce cannot hold back tears as his mother reads his report card.

"I tried. I did everything she said, but I couldn't get those sentences right."

He is ten years old, and he cares. He cares about letting his parents down, and he cares about what his friends think, and he cares too that his A in social studies does not compensate for his failure in English.

Bruce works as hard as most ten-year-olds. He prefers football after school or fishing with his dad on weekends, but he is earnest. He never plays with his shell collection or works on a model airplane until his homework is done. He even skipped television for the week of his science project.

He hates English, though, and Mrs. Sills, his teacher, as well. She assigns a story to be written and gives him a D because he misspells four words, even when all that part about the space station is so good. When he gets mixed up between adverbs and adjectives, Mrs. Sills makes him stay after school and write one hundred times, "Adverbs modify verbs; adjectives modify nouns." But she never explains what "modify" means.

Mrs. Sills wrote only two comments on Bruce's report card. One said, "Miss Keene finds Bruce interested in social studies." The other said, "Bruce should get tutoring in English."

"I guess we'll have to find a tutor," his mother agrees as she reads the comment. A tear, rolling down Bruce's cheek, hangs from his chin. He wipes it away with the back of his hand, streaking his face with dirt.

"She's a terrible teacher, and I hope she drowns," Bruce blurts out. His mother sends him to his room until his father comes home.

Neither his mother nor his father considers the possibility that Bruce may be right about his teacher.

Lisa tries to hide her report card when it arrives, but her mother finds it in a desk drawer under a picture of Cheryl Ladd. She calls Lisa, and together they go over her marks: *English—D. Math—F. French—D. History—D. Art—B. Physical Education—Incomplete.* A general comment across the bottom of the page reads, "Lisa contributes very little to the class and shows no interest in her work. She must apply herself more vigorously if she wants to see any progress."

Her mother reads the comment aloud, recalling the favorable comments teachers used to write in elementary school. What could have happened in two years?

Lisa is in eighth grade—a square-shaped girl with long hair. What used to be blond is now "dirty brown." It falls from a center part down her face like a curtain behind which she hides. Over her blue jeans she wears one of her brother's shirts—long and loose so that no one can tell there is a figure beneath. She keeps on her wool ski jacket, the hood halfway over her head. Last month Lisa's parents attended a teacher conference at school and learned that Lisa's I.Q. tested at 103.

"My God, Mark's is 132," her father gasped.

"Well," the teacher assured him, "you can't always predict these things."

Now that they know, Lisa's parents stop pushing her, and the teacher does, too. They expect little.

"So what?" her mother says. "She's a nice girl. She'll be a good wife and mother."

"Not unless she meets a man with tunnel vision who can see what she looks like," her father jokes. "Come to think of it, what *does* she look like?"

Her mother looks at her now as she holds the report card. I guess she's at an awkward age, she tells herself. Aloud she says, "Who cares about an old report card, anyway? Run along and play."

Lisa retreats to her room, closes the door, and sits looking at the wall. Her mother hasn't noticed that Lisa hasn't played in over a year.

Identifying the Problem

The four students just described are real. Each of them has an academic problem in school. Each of them has parents who care and teachers who should care. Yet no one examines their problems or even faces them or attempts to discover solutions. By senior year in high school, Bob and Lisa will have dropped out; Edna will still be getting D's and F's. Only Bruce will graduate and go to college, but no thanks to his parents for that.

The problems these four students have represent the four main kinds of academic problems with which parents and children have to cope:

1. Edna *has low ability and possible minimal brain damage.* She is not capable of doing better work in a normal school situation.

2. *Bob exerts no effort.* So set has his pattern become that under existing conditions he never will exert effort.

3. *Bruce has a poor teacher.* Under her inept guidance, he will not be able to learn. Only when he gets more capable teachers will his educational future be saved.

4. *Lisa has an emotional problem.* The burden of her inner turmoil prevents her from learning at the level of her ability.

None of these young people's parents looks beyond the academic problems indicated on the report card. They see only bad marks, which they accept at face value, all but destroying their children in the process. They read only superficial teacher comments, in which they place their faith.

One of the horrors of education today is that parents accept without question what teachers tell them about their children.

Reading that statement, some parents may instantly respond, "Good, I knew John didn't deserve a D." However, refusing to accept what teachers say is not the same as arguing over marks. Marks are coincidental. They symbolize an achievement level with no regard to its cause. Teacher's comments, however, are intended to probe beneath the marks into a student's motivation and feelings. As clues to academic problems, they are significant and should be questioned. To the detriment of their children, the parents of Edna, Bob, Bruce, and Lisa concerned themselves only with marks. Important signs of trouble, which were not observed and not communicated by teachers, were overlooked by the parents as well.

As all parents can, they could have discovered significant clues to existing problems from other sources.

The children themselves can provide clues. None of the parents in our case studies tried to discover from their own child what was at the root of the academic difficulty. They could have asked—and there are ways of asking, as discussed in chapter 4.

In addition, they could have observed. Changes in dress, in study habits, in after-school activities, in social relationships can indicate inner thoughts and feelings. Parents can learn to see such changes and to help their children see them, too.

The school also provides clues. Most teachers pass off a one-sided comment as an evaluation of a child. With so many students to evaluate, the comment is likely to be not only one-sided but superficial as well. And without time for a great deal of thought, the teacher will usually write something that is safe and general.

Therefore, parents and their children would do well to follow through with a three-way conference on any report card that indicates a problem. If the teacher resists including the student, the parent should insist. It is a parent's right to have the child present at a conference with the teacher.

The three-way conference puts the problem on the table with no possibility of anyone's misunderstanding. Once understood, the problem is en route to being solved.

Outside sources can help to identify problems as well. If the problem is such that the child alone is not aware of its nature and that the child, teacher, and parent combined cannot grasp it, the parent must seek outside help. The initial need is to diagnose the problem:

Is it a problem of ability? What is the child's I.Q.? Verbal and numerical levels? Reading comprehension and speed? Visual, spatial, and abstract abilities? Can the child relate things? Draw conclusions? Follow a sequence?

Is it a medical problem? Does the child have poor eyesight? Bad hearing? Is there a thyroid problem? Anemia? Does the child eat properly?

Is it a neurological problem? Is there minimal brain damage? Is there a left-right vision reversal? Are there forms of aphasia?

Is it a psychological problem? Is the child having emotional difficulties? Is the family system as a whole failing to work constructively?

Finding a Solution

Once an academic problem has been diagnosed, all concerned—parents, teachers, children, and sometimes professionals—should join together to find a solution. Occasionally parents are embarrassed by a problem their children have, feeling that it reflects on them negatively. Trying to save face, they may attempt to hide it from the school. Yet hiding it precludes solving it. The shame lies not in the problem but only in their vanity.

Parents can effect great reverses in their children's academic performance after diagnosis when they cooperate with the professional source and the school to devise a plan of action.

If the problem is low ability, parents can:

• Alleviate pressure for achieving higher grades. Pushing will not make for better marks; it will make the child unhappy and probably neurotic. In severe cases, transfer to a less demanding class may be necessary.

• Seek areas other than academic ones in which the child can achieve. Academics are only *one* area of school achievement— unfortunately, the one on which parents and teachers place most emphasis. However, parents should try to find others in which the child has strengths and can meet with success— sports, the arts, human relationships.

• Reinforce the value of the child as a whole person, not as a mere mark-getter. Know, and let the child know, that this person is worth far more than any quarterly report card.

If the problem is lack of effort, parents can:

• Set up conditions more conducive to studying at home. Regulate television viewing, make sure that the child has privacy, and see that the necessary equipment is available.

• Help the child outline a study plan that will budget time well. Do not make the plan yourself.

• Let the child face the results of failure to work. Do not nag, do not do the work yourself, do not make excuses, do not blame the school. Let the child who does not work accept responsibility for the consequences.

If the problem is poor teaching, parents can:

• Recognize it as a possibility only after careful investigation. Do not use poor teaching as a cover-up for your child's failures.

• Discuss it with your child—not as an excuse, not as an activist cause, but as a fact of life.

• Supplement the teaching situation at home. Chapter 3 gives specific details on ways to do this.

• Consider attempting to remove the teacher if other parents have similar experiences and share your feelings. Chapter 9 offers suggestions and guidelines for this eventuality.

If the problem is physical, parents can:

• Seek treatment from a pediatrician or an internist. A physical checkup by your family physician is the best starting point. Your doctor knows the child and can eliminate many possibilities.

• Seek treatment from a specialist—eye doctor, ear doctor, and such. Your family doctor may refer you to a specialist if the examination does not reveal anything or if a problem is suspected.

• Seek treatment from a neurologist. There may be a problem in the central nervous system which can be treated.

• Seek treatment through diet. More and more nutritionists are working with young people, prescribing diets that affect general behavior and learning.

If the problem is emotional, parents can:

• Have the child go to a psychologist, who will help the child develop coping techniques.

• Have the child go to a psychiatrist, who will work with the child in greater depth to uncover causes of the emotional disorder.

• Let the family join the child for family therapy under the guidance of a psychologist.

• Let the child enter group therapy. This will consist of a group of people who help themselves by sharing their problems with each other. The group is usually led by a professional.

• Take the child to a child development center. This is an agency, usually nonprofit, that studies the whole child, approaching from all dimensions at once. Treatment may include interviews with a psychologist, neurological training, and diet, for instance.

Dealing with the Problems

Let us turn back time for Edna, Bob, Bruce, and Lisa. Let us wave a magic wand, endowing their parents with the insight and wisdom they lacked. And let us give them another chance to react to the report cards they opened.

"You look unhappy," Edna's father says. "Did you expect better grades?"

Edna nods.

"It hurts, I know," he continues.

"I tried," Edna says. "I did the best I could, but I just can't get that stuff. Not the way Al does."

"Al's a different person. Let's talk about you. I hate to see you so unhappy. What do you think we can do?"

Edna looks up hopefully. "Could you talk to my teachers about it?"

"We could both talk to your teachers."

Edna and her father meet with her teachers. Checking her records, they find low scores. However, the tests were group-given and therefore not highly accurate. They arrange for Edna to take a battery of individual tests—"to see what kind of program you can get more out of," says one of her teachers.

After the results are in, the school administration transfers Edna to a less challenging English class and to remedial math.

"Let's keep her in history," her father injects. "She likes it."

Edna drops French and takes an extra art course instead. She is proud to show her father two of her paintings hanging in the hall.

With a modified program, Edna finishes high school. She enters art school, aiming at a career in commercial art. More important, she begins to like herself as she stops meeting failure on her father's terms and meets success on her own.

Bob's father frowns as he reads the report card. Bob pretends to burst into tears.

"Cut the clowning, Bob," his father says. "Remember you and I made a bargain."

Bob looks surprised.

"Have you forgotten? If you received another bad report, you and I were going to talk with Miss Nutley and see what could be done," his father continues. "Well, you got it again. Let's go."

"What do you want to see old Nuthead for?" Bob begins. His father cuts him off.

They sit down with Miss Nutley and with Bob's other teachers. His father puts the responsibility squarely on him.

"I want you to know," he tells the teachers, "that Bob's

work is his responsibility. If he fails, he fails. But his mother
and I will stand behind the school on whatever consequences he
has to take because of his failure."

Bob continues to fool around and make excuses. His parents say nothing. At the end of the next semester, he has failed
two subjects. His teachers insist on summer school if he is to return in the fall.

"Are you kidding? Summer school? I've planned a trip to
my cousin's in California." He looks to his father for confirma-
tion. None is forthcoming.

Bob goes to summer school, angry, feeling that the world is
against him. But next fall he begins to do homework at night.
His parents no longer encourage television; he joins them when
his work is done. When he backslides, he is forced to assume responsibility: he loses a weekend by waiting till the last minute to
write a source paper. His parents go off skiing without him.

Eventually, he graduates from high school and from college,
and when he is married and a father himself, he is as aware of
what his children are or are not doing as his father was.

Bruce's mother and father are more concerned when Bruce
has to stay after school and write one hundred sentences. They
question Mrs. Sills, who justifies herself with, "He needs discipline, and if he didn't know what 'modify' meant, he *should*
have."

When they read her suggestion for a tutor on the report
card, they question Bruce. "Do you think you need a tutor?"

"The whole class needs one, Mom. She never explains
things—honest. She just makes us copy from our books and
keep our desks neat."

Bruce and his parents see Mrs. Sills. She is angry, accusing
them of spoiling Bruce. "It won't hurt him to write a hundred
sentences, you know."

They ask Mrs. Sills for materials so they can work with
Bruce at home. She gives them a few— reluctantly—and Bruce's
parents have to make their own materials for the rest of the
year.

They explain to their son that even adults are sometimes

not good at their jobs. They do not get angry, nor do they deride the teacher. They simply make sure that Bruce understands his work. They find him bright and eager to learn.

They discuss Mrs. Sills with the PTA president, who has had other complaints, and she finally approaches the principal. After investigating, the principal transfers Mrs. Sills to a position with materials development, where she will not be working with children. (She is tenured and cannot be fired.)

In sixth grade, Bruce has an exciting teacher. He makes the year even more exciting by continuing to share it with his parents at home.

By the time Lisa receives her report card, her mother and father have had long discussions. They worry about her appearance—how it has changed into the tent look, under which she seemed to crawl. They worry that she has become a loner, dropping her old friends and sitting alone in her room most of the time. And they worry that she has lost interest in school.

"I know you're unhappy, Lisa," her mother says. "I've seen it for a long time. Is it something we can talk about?"

Lisa shakes her head.

"You're afraid we won't understand?" her mother questions.

Lisa shrugs.

"Maybe we won't," her mother continues, "because so many things are happening inside people your age that even *you* don't understand." Lisa remains silent. "Would it help to talk to someone else about the way you feel?"

Lisa agrees to see a therapist. After her parents advise the school, her guidance counselor contacts the therapist, filling him in on details she and Lisa have discussed at school. Lisa is thirteen and hates herself. She is a confused mass of contradictions. Shapeless and stringy-haired, she dreams of being Cheryl Ladd. Despising boys, she longs for them to like—even tease—her the way they do some of the girls. Loving her parents, she wants to be away from them; she wants to be away from her classmates, away from school, away from everybody. In her heart she is lonely.

Lisa cannot concentrate on academics, not with such chaos inside. She cannot even take a valid I.Q. test. She thinks there is something wrong with her.

But after eight months of psychotherapy and a year of group therapy, she is now fifteen, wears a bra, and has begun to go out with boys. Her I.Q. tests 126 the following year.

Guidelines for Action

Parents can turn the troubled lives of their children into positive learning experiences, just as the parents of Edna, Bob, Bruce, and Lisa did the second time around. If you think your child has academic problems, here are some suggested guidelines to steer you in the right direction.

1. Do not get angry. Your anger over low marks will magnify, not eradicate, the problem.

2. Discuss the problem with your child. Find out whether he or she is aware of a problem at all. Try to determine its cause. (Rereading chapter 4 may help you learn how to elicit the information.)

3. Find out how your child feels about doing poorly in school.

4. See whether you can come up jointly with a solution to the problem—new study habits, less TV, parental help, etc.

5. If the problem is too serious to effect a change, together discuss it with the teachers.

6. Do not accuse the teachers. Do not be angry at them. Do not pass the buck to them. Ask them for help.

7. Let your child assume responsibility for following through on whatever help the teachers provide.

8. Do not nag about what has been decided on. By doing it, your child accepts the credit; by not doing it, the failure. Do not take either away.

9. Support the school in holding your child accountable for meeting the terms agreed on with the teachers—even though you may be inconvenienced. A slight inconvenience at this point may save a great deal of pain later on—for both of you.

Academic problems are endemic to your child's school experience. Remember, though, that they are soluble when you adhere to the adage that the best way out of a problem is through it.

BEHAVIOR PROBLEMS

Mrs. Martin was thrilled to attend her oldest child's first open house at school. Proudly she introduced herself to the kindergarten teacher: "I'm Bill Martin's mother."

The teacher frowned, then smiled reassuringly. "He'll be all right. He seems to be behaving better already. Don't worry."

"No, I think you have misunderstood," repeated the young mother. "I'm *Bill Martin's* mother."

"Yes." The teacher had understood.

Many parents, like Mrs. Martin, send an angel from home to become a demon in school. Others find the situation reversed.

Mrs. Caldwell lived for the day when the child who drove her crazy would depart for six hours of learning in school and of peace and quiet at home. She slinked into the opening PTA meeting, hoping for a chance to apologize, and was met by a beaming teacher.

"What a joy your daughter is!"

Mrs. Caldwell looked down to see whether she had pinned on the wrong name tag. Her Dr. Jekyll dwells in school; her Mr. Hyde at home.

Still a third, different situation arises, as it did in an affluent Westchester suburb, in which both home and school see a beautiful child, and yet . . .

Mindy was the idol of her school and of her parents— bright, popular, alert, and eager. She was a cheerleader, a star in school plays, a top student, even an athlete. Her mother counted her blessings, wearing her pride with only a minimum of smugness.

One day the manager of a local department store phoned the principal to say that he had caught seven girls shoplifting. The principal drove downtown, finding Mindy and six other cheerleaders waiting in the manager's office. No mother could have been more stunned to receive the principal's phone call; no principal more stunned to have to make it.

Why had Mindy and the other girls taken to shoplifting—not once, but on a weekly basis all year? Guidance counselors and the school psychiatrist talked with the girls and their parents, uncovering reasons ranging from the effects of television to mass hysteria.

Mindy herself gave the most convincing reason: "I couldn't stand being so damned good any more."

The lesson to be learned from Mindy and from the Martin and Caldwell kindergarteners is simply this: Every child has a potential for getting into trouble at school—the good child, the wild child, and the perfect child. When parents accept this fact, they allow their children to be normal—neither paragons nor monsters—and spare themselves possible shock in the future.

The assorted behavior problems parents have to face, ranging from A for apathy to Z for zealotry, fall into three main areas: problems at school, at home, and in the community. Most often they are interrelated.

Problems of Behavior in School

Among younger children, *aggressiveness* is the most common teacher complaint. A child throws a block or breaks up other children's games or hits them. Many a classmate has a bloody nose as proof; many a teacher, a black-and-blue shin.

Both parents and teachers panic over a so-called uncontrollable child, the former fearing for the safety of their children, the latter for the safety of their job. Their control threatened, they often attack with accusations. Parents may begin with a phone campaign, blaming the teacher for overpermissiveness.

"We need a teacher in there who can keep these kids in line," they say, stirring up other parents.

The teacher, on the other hand, is likely to complain to the principal that it is impossible to do anything with the aggressive child because of parental spoiling and lack of cooperation with the school.

The result is that people, not problems, get attacked. People grow angry, and the problem goes right on existing.

The second most common teacher complaint against young children is, *"That child won't sit still a minute!"* Often the parent has a similar problem at home but may conceal it in a defensive counterattack on the teacher.

The child may actually be hyperactive—a bona fide term grossly abused as a catchall for misbehavior. Truly hyperactive (or hyperkinetic) children are unable to control themselves; they *have* to jump up in the middle of a story and run around; they *have* to reach over and poke a neighbor; they *have* to disobey the teacher's order to stand quietly in line.

Both parents and teachers used to despair of hyperactivity, hoping only to survive until the child outgrew it, until Dr. Benjamin Fein came along with a new treatment that has calmed thousands of children without drugs. His experiments with diet show a direct ratio between sugar and food additives and hyperkinetic behavior. Now both he and child centers across the country test and treat children "who won't sit still a minute." According to the Child Development Institute in New York, which combines diet with exercise, they have an almost 100 percent success rate in calming hyperactive children.

Not every jumpy child is hyperactive, however. Some are simply uncontrolled—spoiled, as the teacher prefers saying. Parents can easily develop such a child, as every grandparent knows. They let the child interrupt while they are speaking; they say "no" and then let the child's whining change their mind; they give in to whatever a nagging child wants; they lay down a rule and let the child break it at will. Then at age six or seven, when the child is totally out of control—or, more accurately, totally *in* control of everyone around—they seek desperately for a reason for such behavior, other than the poor job they have done. Hyperactivity becomes the scapegoat.

A third behavior problem common among young children is *disruptiveness*. If not arrested, it continues into junior high school and high school, becoming a modus operandi. The child clowns in class, gaining little respect but much laughter from peers, in first grade making faces like a monkey behind the teacher's back; in fifth grade feigning the hiccups; in junior high swaggering to the podium in an exaggerated way to read a report; in high school embarrassing the teacher with a personal question.

When confronted by the teacher, this child pleads innocence: "I didn't do anything. I can't help it if I have the hiccups ... if I walk that way ... if I have a question." When questioned by Mother or Father, the child becomes a persecuted victim: "She always picks on me for nothing." Once again the problem of behavior is buried under personal attacks, never to be resolved.

As children grow older, the nature of school problems takes a more serious turn. No longer are they openly disruptive, but subtler, more insidious. *Rule breaking* is the common behavior problem in school. The student sneaks into the lavatory to smoke a joint, cuts class to avoid an undone assignment or just to lie in bed, leaves school grounds for lunch, breaks the dress code by going barefoot or braless.

Whatever rule is broken, teachers respond in anger, as if it were a personal attack on them. Parents, usually manipulated by their children, respond protectively. They even lie to cover up their child's misbehavior. One mother tells the school nurse that her daughter is sick in bed when she has actually gone to the beach for the day. Another invents a dietary reason for her son to "come home for lunch" when he is in fact at McDonald's. The problem is lost in the whitewash.

Vandalism is a growing problem, with cities across the nation spending millions of dollars a year to repair damage. At the simplest level students scratch their names and favorite words into walls. At a more serious level, they break windows, destroy files, and set fire to classrooms.

It is difficult to apprehend vandals, for they seek quiet times and unpopulated spots for their efforts. Schools double their guard staff and urge city police to reroute prowl cars around the schools. Principals give pep talks to the student body, accompanied by threats, in an effort to quell destruction. Parents demand tougher policies, certain that their children "would never do that." But as the television spot asks, "It is ten o'clock. Do you know where your children are?" From the looks of the growing problem, there are a number of parents who do not.

More serious than vandalism is increasing *violence* within

schools: stealing, rape, assault, even murder. In some schools, children are afraid to use lavatories, and teachers dare not walk in the halls alone. So enormous is the problem that it cannot be considered misbehavior; it is crime. Parents, teachers, and administrators throw up their hands, disclaiming responsibility. Yet they are the schools; they are the children's leadership. If they abandon responsibility and deny accountability, who is left to accept it? The community? They are also the community.

Truancy is the most widespread behavior problem in schools. Each day four and a half million young people who should be in school are roaming the streets, perhaps committing the crimes for which home and school refuse to take responsibility. Truancy is the parents' responsibility. How can they avoid assuming it when the highest absenteeism rate is in kindergarten? When Monday and Friday are the biggest absentee days? When children with older truant siblings tend to become truants too? When high absenteeism comes from children who are kept home to help with family work?

On the other hand, how can teachers avoid assuming responsibility when student absenteeism exists in direct ratio to teacher absenteeism? When children in nonenrichment programs are the most frequent truants? When truancy increases as the school year wears on? When absenteeism is highest on gym days?

Problems of Behavior at Home

Rule breaking in school has its corollary at home: *disobedience.* The small child is told not to cross the street and does it. The preteen is told to wash the dishes and doesn't do it. The junior high student is told to do homework before watching TV and skips the homework. The high schooler is told not to take the car and takes it.

Disobedience can become a pattern for children. Parents may moan but feel powerless. "I can't do a thing with him," they sigh as little Johnny takes a cookie from the cookie jar when he has been told not to—or as big Johnny takes the family car when he has been informed that his parents need it.

Irresponsibility is another behavior problem that often

arises at home. Parents see it as rule breaking because they hear themselves order children to "take responsibility." When their children fail to comply, parents view their irresponsibility as disobedience: "You didn't do what I told you to do."

Responsibility, however, is not a rule to be kept or broken. It is, in educator John Dewey's words, "a development of the mind." Children do not learn it through lecture but rather through example and experience. That child learns who is given the opportunity to *experience* the result of his or her responsible behavior and see the *example* of the parents' responsible behavior.

This lesson is not always granted a child, however. For instance, parents may nullify the experience of undone homework by nagging and pushing the child into doing it—or in some cases, by doing it themselves. At the same time, they are removing the example of responsibility through their own irresponsible behavior in taking over. The child is left, then, with neither experience nor the example from which to learn a lesson of responsibility—and in addition, with the blame for not learning.

Problems of Behavior in the Community

While the single child at home may be a law-abiding citizen, the same child may run amok in a group. The group overturns ash cans on Halloween. The group slashes tires. The group gets drunk after a football game. The group has a pot party.

Most parents find it difficult to believe their child capable of misbehavior within the community. Whether it is something as minor as playing the stereo too loud at a party after midnight or as major as robbery, parents tend to seek reasons, excuses, and scapegoats. The peer group serves as all three. Sighing over Billy's misconduct, parents can say, "If only he had different friends."

They do not realize that the parents of Billy's friends are saying the same thing. Children select their peer groups; they don't get dragged into them unwillingly. Billy *is* his peer group. Parents should be aware of this when a problem arises and, instead of damning their child's friends and classmates, look to their own child first.

Behavior problems can be used as opportunities for children, parents, and even communities to learn. For learning seldom takes place in stasis, and misconduct is a good stirrer.

Children can learn valuable lessons: They can learn that their actions do not end with them but can hurt countless others, many of whom they do not even know. They can learn that they are in control of their actions, that they alone make the decision to do or not to do. They can learn that others judge them from their actions—not as daring and clever as they see themselves in their misbehavior but as weak and thoughtless. Lastly, they can learn that people—their parents and sisters and brothers and neighbors—care about their loved ones and their homes and their community. These are lessons to make a young person grow.

Parents can learn from their child's misbehavior, too. They can see their own responsibility or carelessness or ignorance. They can see the need for help—from school and community, perhaps from members within their own families. And they can see what love is—not the pride of showing off a child's accomplishments but the support given in a child's failure.

For its own part, the community can assume responsibility and offer alternatives—a youth center, an active library, a theater project, day camps, enrichment programs, and summer school. It can also learn that delinquent children are not "bad" but troubled, and it can seek alternatives to punishment in order to help.

Everyone can learn from a behavior problem if steps are taken—not if the problem is hidden or a scapegoat is found or responsibility is denied. Parents are in the best position to initiate steps, to see that they are taken, and to take them themselves.

Guidelines for Action

Here are some suggested guidelines to help you head step by step toward positive action. If your child is facing a behavior problem:

1. Talk about it. Do not pretend that it does not exist.
2. Speak reasonably and lovingly. Do not scold or moralize.

3. Help assume responsibility for it. If your child lays the blame on others, point out that the decision to act belonged to no one else. To the words, "But everyone did it. It's not fair that I got caught," point out that you are not concerned with "everyone." "Everyone" does not alter the fact that your child was involved.

4. Try to discover the reason for the actions. What did your child hope to gain, a material thing such as money, or a sense of well-being, or status with the crowd? How did your child feel while engaged in this misconduct?

5. Figure out together what should be done now. How can the harm caused others be repaid? An apology? Work? Money? How can your child learn not to misbehave again? Be deprived of something? Do a project? Get professional help?

6. If the school is involved in the misconduct, as in the case of the cheerleaders, further steps need to be taken. Talk with the school—teacher, principal, and/or guidance counselor—and with your child about what happened. Do not attack. Do not defend. Discuss without judging.

7. Let the child and the school try to uncover reasons for what happened: Did the school situation foster it? Did the child bring it on alone?

8. Decide what can be changed to ensure its not happening again, both within the school—different scheduling, less free time, more challenging classes, less pressure, more supervision, etc.—and within the student—new routine, new attitude, help from a counselor, etc.

9. Decide what disciplinary measure the school should take, to make reparation, and to rehabilitate the student. If the young person's misconduct has involved the larger community, community representatives must also be included in the discussion. If it is a behavior problem that is against *school rules* as well as against *community laws,* such as smoking pot in school, parents, student, school, and community should talk together. If, however, the misconduct is limited to the community and does not involve the school, such as stealing a car or breaking store windows, the school should be excluded from discussion.

Nothing does more damage than involving every aspect of a

child's life in punishment for wrongdoing. When the school has not figured in the misconduct, either as a locale for it or as the peer group that was part of it, parents, community, and young person should handle the problem alone. There will be more than enough people judging and criticizing without adding teachers and friends. If the child's reputation is clean at school, let it remain so. Parents may understand this better if they ask themselves how they would feel if every time they got a speeding ticket, they had to discuss it with their boss.

10. There are two final steps for parents to take in handling behavioral problems. The first is to help your child understand the reason for the discipline: because it is important to learn the lesson of cause and effect and because you care. Doing nothing about bad behavior would be easier and less risky—you would remain the "nice guy." But caring parents work and risk because their child is worth it.

11. Finally, let your child be sure of your love. In the midst of problems and disciplinary measures, loving may be forgotten. Years ago while a student at Mount Holyoke, I heard Robert Frost say, "You've got to love what's lovable and hate what's hateable. It takes brains to see the difference." Have brains. Your child is not a dream of perfection you have invented but a human being with strengths and weaknesses—like you—a human being to love.

SOCIAL PROBLEMS

Bonnie Brown keeps to herself. At fifteen, she writes poetry and avoids school parties. "I think the kids are boring," she tells her father, who keeps urging her to go. She prefers to ride her bicycle or walk through nearby woods looking for birds. Sometimes when she comes home from school she likes to sit in her blue rocker and look out the window. It makes her feel peaceful.

"That kid has a problem," Mr. Brown tells his wife.

In fact, Bonnie's father is the one with the problem.

Bonnie is happy. She is the "strange little thing" in school with no real friends or enemies, who drifts in and out of class like a moth. She does her work, passes with average marks, struggles through gym class, and spends her free time working on weird projects in the lab. Teachers and students alike accept her as she is—so different as to be nonthreatening—for there is no possibility of making her conform.

Bonnie's father is unhappy. He has a stereotyped idea of daughters which Bonnie does not match, no matter how hard he tries. So to him she is a threat. She is not pretty and does not seem to care. She is not popular and is glad.

"You could fix yourself up," he says. "You'd be a knockout. There'd be phone calls from boys then, I bet."

"I don't want to," she answers.

"Why not, for God's sake?"

"I'm happy this way."

And she is. Bonnie has no social problems.

Alice down the block has a social problem.

She too is different. She will be pretty some day, but now she is too tall and too thin—a potential basketball player if she were better coordinated. She is a great math student, undertaking constant independent study so she will not get bored in class. The English teacher loves her because she reads four books to everyone else's one.

But Alice is unhappy. At sixteen she has never had a date or even been asked to a school dance. She goes alone sometimes and hangs around, but no one dances with her. The girls in her class consider her a bore. And the boys ignore her—until they want to copy homework.

Alice is unhappy. Rejected by the crowd, she buries her hurt in academic success and keeps trying to belong. That is where she differs from Bonnie, and that is why she has a social problem. *A social problem is not defined by the parents' sense of failure over having an "unpopular" child; it is the child's unhappiness over peer relations.*

Not every student is a prom queen or team captain. Students who win these honors win them by virtue of qualities that reflect peer group values. In schools such as New York's Bronx High School of Science the values are intelligence and academic achievement, stemming from the students' orientation. In many other schools across the country, however, values are formed from movie stars or role models on television—Farrah Fawcett and Lee Majors, Donnie Osmond and Marie. The young people reflecting them are smiling and beautiful and smooth, like the Barbie and Ken dolls on which they were raised. While no law precludes a prom queen's being intelligent, even in this age of dawning enlightenment, most teenage boys evaluate looks and personality more highly than brains.

At the other extreme are students like Bonnie, who live untouched by the in crowd. They seem not to need them. These are happy loners, the "interesting" children who surprise everyone by growing up to be Eleanor Roosevelt or Albert Einstein. They will probably be voted "Most Unusual" rather than "Most Likely to Succeed," but their futures may lead them in directions every bit as noteworthy as that of the boy headed for Harvard who is certain to become a senator.

In between are the Alices of school, striving to be accepted, trying again and again as they fail. Their happiness lies in joining the in crowd, and so they imitate them. They dress like them, restyle their hair, hang around them. For their efforts they are often laughed at and rejected.

Alice will graduate an unwilling loner. Others are more fortunate; they find each other. They form subgroups from which they draw sustenance. They belong at last, easily rationalizing away their failure to belong to the winning group; those kids are no good, stuck-up, wild. Furthermore, they reinforce themselves by rejecting classmates still less accepted than they—Janet, for instance.

Eventually everyone in the class finds a place—either functioning in a group or outside, alone. Of the latter, some cope, others suffer. It is the sufferers who have a social problem because they fail to adjust to the reality of themselves or of their classmates but live in a make-believe world of self-loathing and other-idolizing. They see themselves as ugly, dumb, awkward, and uninteresting; they see others as beautiful, graceful, bright, and charming.

Without knowing it, parents often increase their child's low self-image: for example, in their efforts to make a daughter popular, they arrange blind dates, which she cannot handle, or plan parties, which no one attends. Their pushing increases her sense of inadequacy as she cries within herself, "See? Even my parents know what a failure I am."

Louise's mother meant well when she persuaded her son's friend to take Louise to a dance. Poor Louise—overweight and pasty, with nothing to say and the charmlessness that comes from knowing it. Her mother bought her a new dress, curled her hair, and put lipstick on her. Insensitive to her daughter's anxiety, she sent her off with instructions to open her eyes wide and smile as she danced.

Louise tried. But next day it was all over school that she had had a stomachache at the dance.

"Boy," her date said, "she rolled her eyes like a sick cow."

Louise's mother wanted to help but was incapable of offering what Louise really needed—understanding and support. She could see no further than her own need, which was to have a popular daughter. Like Amanda in Tennessee Williams's *The Glass Menagerie,* she could not look *at* her own daughter; she could only look *through* her into a distortion of her own dreams. Gentleman callers and blind dates cannot build relationships with dreams.

Unfortunately, most parents are as helpless as Louise's mother in facing social problems with a child because they see them not as *problems* but as *failures.* Unpopular children are failures; even worse, their parents are failures. And that is where it hurts. In a desperate move to undo the failure—to ease their pain and guilt—they overreact, intensifying the problem that existed in the first place.

Finding the Causes

If parents would instead confront the difficulty, laying their egos aside, they could begin to help their child. The first step is to discover why the problem exists. Let's consider five major underlying causes.

Appearance

The great American ideal is conformity: everyone wants to look like everyone else. The 48-billion-a-year cosmetic industry testifies to this, in its standardizing of the color of hair, lips, and eyelids, of the shape of hairdos, of everybody's smell. Mass-produced copies of designer originals testify as well. Even the so-called rebels who reject the mainstream look turn to jeans and beards and long, antiqued skirts and end up looking like each other just the same. They want to. That is how they feel accepted.

The same holds true for schoolchildren. Not having that "right" look is the most blatant reason for rejection. Mary Ann's mother sent her to school in seventh grade with braids hanging down her back, and her classmates laughed. Jack's mother kept stuffing him with sweets, and he was known in school as Fatso. A slight deviation in manner of dress can cause the problem—skirts too long, trousers too short, the wrong brand of blue jeans, hand-knitted sweaters, brown oxfords.

Physical Defects

Until 1978, when school systems were mandated to mainstream the handicapped, few children had ever had contact with a physically handicapped child. Conformity was complete: not only did classmates dress and comb their hair alike, they were all physically perfect—seeing eyes, two legs, and strong, straight backs.

Today, however, classrooms mix so-called normal children at least part of the day with paraplegics, with the blind and deaf, with those who have cerebral palsy, and even with the mentally retarded. These children are now referred to as "special," not handicapped; but even a mandate cannot convince us that it is all right to be less than perfect.

Just as the Civil Rights Act could not legislate people to accept blacks into their lives—only into their buses and restaurants—neither can mainstreaming make children accept the "specials." In nursery school and kindergarten, yes—for young children are able to see through surface appearances. They accepted blacks long before the Civil Rights Act, until they got older and their parents and teachers convinced them they were wrong.

Once the awareness of conformity settles on them, however, children look askance at anyone different, anyone less perfect than they are. They tease "Four Eyes" about his glasses and feel uncomfortable around Jane with her hearing aid. They avoid the blind child, try not to stare at the paraplegic in his wheelchair, make fun of cleft palate speech, and are simply terrified of a mongoloid.

Given their way, most parents would keep their own child away from different children. That's surely one of the reasons communities fight small group homes for the retarded, resist black or other ethnic families in their neighborhoods, and are as reluctant as they are to spend tax money for ramps and elevators to help the handicapped.

Yet, ironically, their efforts to keep children with "their own kind" turn back on them. Let one of their children turn out to be in any way different, and he or she will be rejected by other parents and children. A speech defect or crossed eyes or a leg brace means that child will be ostracized. Only teeth braces are accepted without questions. Why? Because they are the "in" things—most children wear them.

Social Ineptitude

Social ineptitude cannot be erased by following do-it-yourself steps or by offering incantations to the gods. Which comes first? Is a child awkward because of feeling inadequate, or inadequate because of being awkward? Feeling and action reinforce each other until it no longer matters which is cause and which is effect. It is important only to recognize the problem and to help.

Social ease is learned at home. Children raised in homes where friends come and go grow accustomed to social intercourse; they feel comfortable with people. They like them, and they like themselves.

The socially inept seem to do everything wrong. They trip when walking down the auditorium aisle; they drop their books when talking to a teacher; they blush; they mix up words. They hurt the feelings of others through tactlessness and create anger by being direct. Uncomfortable with people, they avoid them, thus reinforcing their lack of know-how. Or they make jokes about their ineptitude, becoming deliberate clowns: it hurts less to have people laugh *with* you. In either case, they hate themselves.

Value Systems

While parents set their hearts on having a popular child, there are situations in which they might well wish for a reject. Popularity reflects peer values. When those values coincide with the parents' values, they will feel successful over having a popular offspring. The beautiful, the brilliant, the athletic—these are sons and daughters whom parents accept proudly, as the peer group also accepts them.

However, Mindy's group looked up to girls who shoplifted, for they showed courage. Another peer group looked up to the boy who knifed a victim on the street because he showed daring. One group accepts girls only when they have had sexual experience; another accepts boys only after they commit rape. Parents often evaluate behavior according to their own values, which may be far different from those of their children; consider their horror on learning that the third-grade boys formed an in-group based on how far they could urinate out the first-floor lavatory window.

The shock comes in realizing not that a few boys and girls hold what the majority consider deviant moral standards, but that so many boys and girls are willing to abandon their own and their parents' standards to be accepted by the few. The guilt they feel in going against their own beliefs is apparently not as painful as the hurt of being rejected. Popularity is the most desirable thing in the world to them.

"I didn't really want to have sex," a high school junior explained. "But, you know, the kids expected it. What could I do?"

What could she do indeed? With parents pushing their children to be popular—bragging when they are and looking ashamed when they are not—perhaps there was nothing the girl could do. On the other hand, perhaps she could have asked her parents what price she should pay for the popularity they seek. Would her virginity be too high? Her sense of honesty? If parents could see social problems for what they are, perhaps they would ask the questions themselves.

Cultural Differences

America used to be the great melting pot of the world. The goal of immigrants was to be American—the stereotype they read about and saw in movies. In school classmates ridiculed their accents, laughed at their clothing, teased them about lunches in paper bags. So these children wanted nothing more than to become Americanized—accepted.

Today the melting pot is gone. Schools strive to retain bilingualism; fashion picks up ethnic designs; the smallest towns have packaged foods from foreign lands. Even so, the culturally different child is set apart in school. White middle-class America is still the norm, because that is how white middle-class America sees itself.

A tiny black girl was found weeping in the school hall one day. "Jimmy called me black," she sobbed.

"But black is beautiful," the teacher comforted.

The child sobbed even louder. "I'm brown!"

One can only hope that her parents enabled her to see that brown is beautiful too.

After generations of children attend school together and live and play together, perhaps they will learn to accept cultural differences as easily as they do the color of hair. But America will have to learn first, will have to believe—not *pretend* to believe—that it is our differences, not our similarities, that make us strong.

Dealing with the Problems

After exploring the causes of a social problem, you are ready to take the next step: determine what can be done about it.

Some things can be changed. We would all hope to raise children strong enough within themselves to withstand peer rejection—children like Bonnie Brown. "Let the world mock," we would say. "You and I can ignore it, for we are what we are—individuals."

Unfortunately, many children and more parents are unable

to do that. They cannot stand alone against the world, even when the world is no larger than a classroom. Only rebels stand alone, and rebellion is lonely.

On the other hand, when they conform, they relinquish identity. They become robots, and dehumanization is lonely too. The answer lies somewhere between the two. A child who is miserable about not being accepted in school need not be turned into a carbon copy of the other students. Parents can reinforce pride in individuality on major issues, while at the same time helping their child to adapt on the minor ones.

Some causes of nonacceptance can be easily removed. No harm is done by changing a child's way of *dressing*. If classmates laugh at homemade sweaters or too-long skirts, parents can buy sweaters—even secondhand ones if cost is a factor—and turn up hems an inch or two. They do not relinquish their individuality in doing so. If they give up braids or let a son outgrow a bowl haircut, they acquiesce where it does not matter. Life becomes less painful for their child—and no principles are compromised.

Grooming is important to children and can be altered. A dirty child is not accepted, or one with bad skin or body odor or greasy hair. You should be concerned with your child's cleanliness, even if the child is old enough to be personally responsible for it. A suggestion from a parent, an honest word, can possibly improve social relationships. In one school when a parent did not help, a group of boys took a classmate and bathed him themselves. He did not know how to bathe properly; they taught him how.

You can help your children develop ease in conversation by encouraging them in *talking*. The dinner table is a perfect classroom. One family assigns responsibility for the dinner topic to a different child each night. The child prepares ahead from a topic of interest, a book or from a movie or a TV show. This kind of practice gives the children confidence to speak in outside situations.

Another family has a shy daughter who is fearful that she will run out of conversation at a party. She has learned to make a list of possible topics before leaving home, tucking it into her pocketbook. Of course, it is most often unnecessary, but she gains confidence just from knowing it is there.

You can also help your children learn the art of *listening*. A popular boy in school was once voted "The Best Conversationalist." In fact, he spoke very little; he was a great listener. He made other people feel interesting. No wonder his classmates considered him a good conversationalist!

Thoughtfulness is a quality that can be cultivated and helps make friends. The child who shares a chair or passes a Coke or plays a record someone else likes is an asset to a group and will be wanted. You can help your children examine their behavior. Are they selfish—wanting *their* way, filling their needs, telling *their* story? Or are they sensitive to the feelings of others—willing to compromise, helping others have fun, sharing?

Physical appearance can be changed in ways that often free a young person socially. Even when they are not 100 percent successful, they help reshape a child's self-image as well as looks. Contact lenses can replace glasses, showing off pretty eyes. A fat child can be encouraged to reduce; even a few pounds dropped can give the feeling of a new figure. A skinny child can gain weight, and a new sense of masculinity or femininity as well. What is wrong with a fiber-filled bra when a young girl feels that the whole world is staring at her flat chest? It helps temporarily, until she is old enough to realize that her chest size doesn't make any difference. As for a boy, can't barbells or a health club help convert him from a ninety-pound weakling?

A wise mother explained her way of avoiding the generation gap: "I ignored the little things and saved my clout for what mattered." The same advice applies to parental intervention in social problems. Do not exhaust your energies on little things; change them where possible. There will be enough unchangeable ones to challenge you.

Some things cannot be changed. Young people seem more able than their parents to face reality. Children in school can accept the fact that they are poor in math or have low reading comprehension. What is painful for them to accept is their parents' embarrassment over that reality.

If a physical handicap prevents a child's acceptance by others, the fact has to be faced.

"Children don't understand your speech," his mother explained to eight-year-old Timothy, who had a cleft palate. "That's why they laugh or go away. They are embarrassed."

"What can I do about it?" the tearful child asked.

"Let's see. What do you think? Maybe we'll get some ideas together."

They did. Timmy now carries a magic marker with him to write down what his friends can't understand. He also practices speaking before a mirror more arduously than before.

Cindy cannot overcome her handicap as Timmy did. She never will; she is twisted and shaking with cerebral palsy.

"Why did this happen to me?" she used to ask her parents.

"There is no answer, Cindy," they replied. "And it doesn't matter. The fact is it did happen. You hate it, and we hate it, but the fact remains the same."

Cindy explained "the fact" to her classmates in the hope they would be more willing to include her in their fun.

"I know I look funny," she told them. "But inside I'm just like you." Most of her classmates learned that she was right.

Some unchangeables are not physical handicaps but personal differences. One boy writes poetry, another is a Civil War freak, another limits his social life to the Sherlock Holmes club. One girl is an opera buff, another joins the Little League, still a third collects bugs. These are differences to be cherished, even when they set a child apart. Conformity makes life easy; it does not make it colorful.

Still, your child may cry, "Why don't the kids like me?"

A parent can be honest in answering, "Because you are different. That's what is so wonderful about you. You are you—unique and interesting—and we love you."

"Then why don't the kids love me?" the child asks.

"I guess they haven't learned yet that people can be different from each other and still be friends. They'll learn as they grow up."

The greatest difficulty of living in a world of conformity is the pain that comes from being a nonconformist. We are torn:

we want to be ourselves, and we want to be accepted at the same time. You can overcome the difficulty by helping your children change the changeable and live with the unchangeable. You might echo the prayer of Saint Francis: "Grant me, Lord, courage to change what I can, grace to accept what I cannot, and wisdom to know the difference."

Guidelines for Action

In raising children, preventive measures may be taken to avoid social problems. These are common sense, rather than rules to follow, and they are not foolproof.

1. Use your own social life as a role model for your children. As in everything else, children copy what their parents do. If parents are antisocial, chances are that their children will not reach out to make friends. If parents are social climbers, their children can be expected to strive for in-group status. If they are easy and relaxed with friends, their children will probably follow suit.

2. Include your children in social gatherings. Of course, there are times when adults want to enjoy an evening by themselves, leaving children home with a baby-sitter. That is important. It is equally important, however, to expose children to family parties. In this way they will learn to relate to adults as well as to other children, developing social ease across age lines.

3. Include your children's friends in outings. Instead of only the family's going on a picnic or to the zoo, a friend from school should be included at times. The occasion enables parents to observe their children in social situations and lets the children feel that their friends belong in their parents' life as well as in their own.

4. Give parties with your children—on special occasions such as birthdays and even when there is no special occasion. Children develop pride in themselves and in their family when they know their home is a place of welcome and of fun.

5. Participate actively in the child's world—school, scouts, church, etc. Only in this way can children realize that they are important members of the family and that their activities are serious, to their parents as well as to them. When parents be-

come so involved in their own world of business or friends or community that they ignore their child's world, they are saying in effect, "Your interests do not matter to me because mine are better." The child receiving that message can grow up only with a feeling of inadequacy—the root of future social problems.

MORAL PROBLEMS

Samuel Johnson, that critic of literature and lives, wrote, "The morality of an action depends upon the motive from which we act. If I fling a half crown to a beggar with the intention to break his head, and he picks it up and buys victuals with it, the physical effect is good, but with respect to me, the action is very wrong."

Let us see how the act and the intention of students coincide with those of Samuel Johnson. Dishonesty is a common moral problem; let that be the half crown flung to the beggar.

Isabel finds a dollar in the girls' lavatory. Delighted, she pockets it. She adheres to the fourth-grade code of Finders-Keepers.

Kenneth receives a late-night phone call from his best friend, who has not done his math homework and will have to quit the basketball team if his father finds out. Could he copy Kenneth's answers before class in the morning? "Sure."

Ralph has applied to Yale. His midyear grades will carry weight with the admissions office. He steals a copy of the English exam from his teacher's drawer, jots down a few notes, and later looks up and organizes his answers.

Who has acted immorally? Not Isabel, who is truly ignorant of wrongdoing. She did not *take* money; she *found* it. Not Kenneth, whose code of ethics, like that of his friends, puts a higher value on loyalty to friends than on homework. Ralph acted immorally: he commited an act that he knows is wrong in order to expedite his chances of admission to Yale.

Isabel and Kenneth have no guilt with which to cope; Ralph has. Morality is a personal thing. "What is moral," in Ernest Hemingway's words, "is what you feel good after, and what is immoral is what you feel bad after." Isabel and Kenneth feel good. Ralph feels bad.

Isabel needs to learn. Kenneth needs to explore his value system. Ralph needs to solve a moral problem.

Millions of young people in these turbulent times have moral problems to solve—not because they are acting counter to the mores of their parents, but because their acts leave them unhappy. Typical parents, however, miss the moral problems altogether, focusing like a zoom lens on the acts themselves rather than on their children's unhappiness.

For instance, sex throws parents into a panic. No matter what they may know intellectually, emotionally it scares them in relation to their children, whom they often prefer to think of as asexual. In fact, so scary is sex to adults that it has become synonymous with immorality. Cheating, lying, insensitivity, even destructiveness fade in comparison. Immorality is sex—and vice versa.

The girl who is "an easy lay" may sleep around as a means of rebellion against her parents. It works. They look for no causes; they simply scream. The girl who falls in love and has steady sex with one boy is caught by her parents and considered as immoral as the first girl. Her parents make no distinction. They scream too.

Yet the question of morality differs totally for the two girls. The former uses sex for an ulterior motive, thereby using the males with whom she has sex. For her it is a tool to make her parents angry. For the latter, however, sex is an expression of love. It is mutual; it is nonexploitive.

The former girl can be said to have a moral problem, not the latter. Yet the parents of both react similarly.

They rage in shock: "How could you do such a thing!"

They moralize: "Sex without marriage is wrong!"

They lecture: "Boys will no longer respect you!"

They punish: "No more dates for you!"

It cannot be said that their screams fall on deaf ears. The girls hear what they say. What they hear, though, is not the lesson intended; they hear their parents' narrowness, fear, and lack of understanding.

They do not respond by "obeying," of course, by giving up sexual activity and becoming "moral." The first girl grows even angrier, hurt by her parents' unwillingness to look beyond her actions into her needs. They are deaf to her cry for help, and so she seeks still greater revenge and greater solace for her hurts in intensified sexual activity. Over three quarters of a million unwed teenagers became mothers in 1979. One wonders how many pregnancies could have been prevented, not only with the contraceptives and information readily available but with the understanding of parents.

The second girl weeps for her parents' lack of understanding. They besmirch what she holds pure. "Haven't they ever been in love?" If they are unable to empathize, to accept her for what she is and for what she feels, they will lose their daughter. She will leave them, move in with the man, and let the lines of communication break.

Parents can prevent the hurts and tragedies that these two sets of parents brought about if they understand that there are few ultimate *rights or wrongs*—either set forth in a golden book somewhere or imprinted on the minds of their children. Even murder may be considered "right" when it's committed in self-defense. Right and wrong relate to the feelings and thoughts of individuals.

When parents grow to reach this point of understanding, they are in a position to relinquish the role of judge. This done, they can begin to listen to their children, to hear what they say, and to help them as they respond. Until they reach this point, however, judgments will block their hearing and blot out their efforts to help.

Many parents and teachers proclaim that immorality is rampant, meaning sex, drugs, and violence. Many young people feel that immorality is rampant too, meaning something entirely different.

During the Vietnam War, a group of students from a girls' school marched in protest. FUCK WAR! read one banner, held high by a pretty young girl.

"I don't think a nice girl like you should wave such an immoral word around," the school head told her.

"You're right," she admitted. She changed the sign. The administrator said no more when he read the new one: FUCK W—!

Some Possible Causes

It is not difficult to find sources of blame for the increase in moral problems among the young. Psychologists and socialists offer an abundance of them, the following ten being the most credible:

1. The divorce rate continues to increase. With one out of three marriages ending in divorce, young people are becoming disillusioned. Being brought up by single parents, they may also feel less secure.

2. More women are working. With over half the married women in the United States out of the home at jobs all day, children may feel they are being neglected.

3. The federal government has mushroomed in size and bureaucracy and does not appear to be responsive to citizens' desires and needs. Young people thus feel helpless to effect change.

4. Population in America has reached over 230 million. We have seen the effects on young people of the increasing impersonalization of our mass society.

5. Schools are failing. Unable to read or write, kids are unemployable, roaming the streets bored and bitter.

6. Spending is at an all-time high. Young people are brainwashed to want more things; acquisitiveness often can be satisfied only through immoral or illegal acts.

7. Television promotes images of sex and violence. When children grow up on this as a steady diet, their values are eroded.

8. Church attendance has fallen off. When kids abandon religion, they abandon a chief source of the perpetuation of formalized morality.

9. Politics are dishonest. With major Watergates happening each year, young people have lost faith in government and in public integrity.

10. The media avidly publicize what is bad in America. It sells. And the impressionable young, made too aware of the ills and evils around them, "get," as the oldsters say, "ideas."

Although no single one can be held responsible for the

problems of our nation's growth, there is more than a grain of truth in each accusation. Taken together, they represent the forces that shape our young people's lives and with which they have to cope. There are others.

Educators Blame Parents

They have spoiled their children. From fear of not being liked and probably from guilt over not being with them enough, parents have overindulged their offspring. The result is a demand for instant gratification and the inability to cope constructively with its refusal.

They have put excess pressure on their children to succeed. In pushing their children, parents have made them feel acceptable and adequate as human beings only if and when they succeed. Therefore, in the face of failure and weakness, they fall apart. In the face of success, they explode.

Parents Blame Educators

They no longer care about their students. Unions, pensions, vacations, and working conditions take precedence. They strike instead of teaching.

They are too liberal. In democratizing schools, they have destroyed guidelines, giving young people license to run wild.

They are too conservative. In demanding "proper behavior" at the expense of honest expression, they have fostered hypocrisy. In his book *The Finest Education Money Can Buy,* Robert Gaines expresses it this way: "I have seen too many neat, clean-scrubbed and trimmed and Brooks Brothers-attired boys who were vicious bullies in the seclusion of the hall. I have seen too many paragons of courtesy in public who were privately selfish, cynical little snobs."

Some Approaches to Dealing with These Problems

Whatever the cause, wherever lies the responsibility, today's young people are floundering morally. *Why* is a matter of conjecture. *How* is a matter of fact.

It is wise in an exploration of the issue to come to terms

with what morality is. As we have seen, it is *not* a particular behavior. It is *not* a communal code of ethics. It is *not* a specified value. It is a personal thing—a step taken by an individual according to what he or she considers right and wrong.

To teach morality, therefore, is to teach decision-making. If young people are to take moral steps, they must be helped to walk as surely as a baby is helped in learning to take safe steps. Who is there to help them?

Parents. They are prime teachers of morality—and of immorality. Children do not copy what their parents *say;* they copy what they *do.* All the lectures in the world are wasted in teaching morality when a father brags about padding his expense account, calls in sick to his office when he is well, or knifes a competitor in the back. The best-taught lessons go untaught when a mother calls to her daughter from the bedroom, "Tell her I'm not in," pockets 73 cents the supermarket undercharged her, or spreads gossip about a neighbor.

Teachers. They, too, teach morality. The lesson is well remembered when they hint at answers to tests ahead of time, destroy a child in front of the class, speak softly as the principal enters, and yell behind his or her back.

Levels of Morality

Children assimilate moral codes, as plants do liquid, by osmosis. What goes on around them becomes a part of them every day and stays with them far longer than what is told them.

Until recently, moral learning had a mystique about it that few, if any, understood. Harvard's Dr. Lawrence Kohlberg has changed that within the past decade. From his studies of the moral growth of children, he has concluded that there are six levels of morality. Like Piaget, Kohlberg outlines successive levels of learning through which children must go. They cannot skip a level, for they cannot learn the next one until the previous ones have been mastered.

Parents who understand the various levels on the moral ladder are in a better position to know where their children are and to help them deal with their problems:

1. A sense of justice based on obedience. To obey is good; to

disobey is bad. A small child knows right and wrong only by what the parents say. In obeying them, the child does right and feels good; disobeying means feeling bad.

2. A sense of justice in which right action is that which satisfies one's own—and sometimes others'—needs. "I'll do this for you if you do the same for me." Older children begin to gain a sense of give-and-take. A boy will not hit his friend if his friend does not hit him.

3. A sense of justice in which good behavior conforms to what a group expects. Through right action one gains approval. The life of most teenagers centers around group acceptance. Parental standards lose significance as peer standards become the guiding force.

4. A law-and-order sense of justice in which right behavior consists of doing one's duty and following a system of set rules—because they are there. This person adheres to the letter of the law, not thinking things through but following as duty indicates. This is the good soldier, the law-abiding citizen, and often the class president.

5. A sense of justice based on a contract between society and the individual, making life better for all. This may be the student council leader who understands the usefulness of a school constitution or the adult who knows what our country stands for and is proud to stand alongside it.

6. Universal principles of justice, equality, and human rights. Although abstract and usually unwritten, these principles are followed from commitment to and respect for human dignity. This person has understanding transcending law and obedience and like Albert Schweitzer, makes decisions based on respect for life. He or she believes in the Golden Rule, not because it is written in the Bible but because it is written in the heart.

Growth may be arrested at any one of these six levels. Many an adult never grows beyond Level 2: "Bill never did anything for me. Why should I help him out?" Or Level 3: "Let's get a station wagon like the neighbors'." So parents must not expect their children to arrive automatically at the "right" level at the "right" age. There is no such thing.

What is vital for parents to realize is this: *They cannot*

make their child understand morality at a level not yet attained. Four-year-old Eric is a good example. His mother found him one day in the driveway killing ants. Being a strong pacifist, Quaker, and lover of life, she was horrified.

"Don't you know," she pointed out to her young son, "that ants have feelings just like people? You are killing babies whose mothers and fathers will be left lonely and sad."

Eric, concerned over his mother's upset, was quick to explain. "Don't worry, Mom. I'm wiping out whole families."

Eric's mother tried to impose her moral level on him, and it could not work. She acted from Level 6, a respect for life, while Eric understood only Level 1, simple obedience. She would have been more successful had she said simply, "Don't do that. It is wrong."

She might even have tried to raise him to Level 2 with a sense of give-and-take. She might have said, "It is unfair to kill ants. You are so big and they are little. How would you feel if a giant stamped on you?" Eric might have begun to glimpse "an eye for an eye" kind of morality.

No harm was done through the mistaken approach, but this is not always the case. Parents and teachers frequently alienate young people by failing to deal with them at the level on which they are making decisions. "Don't do that; it's wrong" (Level 1) can only antagonize a teenager who is operating from a higher morality.

Mindy and the cheerleaders who were caught shoplifting were operating at Level 3—peer group standards of morality. Their parents dealt with the problem at a variety of levels, most of them unsuccessfully. For instance, some antagonized their children by saying, "You misbehaved; we will punish you" (Level 1). Others talked over the heads of their children: "You have a responsibility to the school even when you are outside; you failed in that responsibility" (Level 5).

Wise parents reached their children at Level 3, where they could understand: "Only a small group of your classmates consider shoplifting admirable. Most of them think it is cheap and dishonest. How are they going to look at you now?" That hit where it hurt.

One father, the wisest of all, used the experience to raise his daughter's moral level from 3 to 4. "Don't you know," he said, "that there are laws bigger than your group of friends at school? Stealing is illegal. People go to jail for it." He helped his daughter not only to solve a moral problem but to grow from it.

Guidelines for Action

Of all children's problems, moral problems are the most difficult for parents to handle because they come closest to undermining the value system on which the parents have built their entire lives. They lie at the core of parent-child relationships, causing more often than any other problem the gap that pulls them apart.

Parents must handle moral problems according to their own value systems. There are, however, a few general rules that apply to everyone, so the following guidelines may be helpful to parents facing moral problems with a child:

If the Problem Is Sexual

1. Don't skirt the issue. State it openly with your child.

2. Listen to the child's feelings and thoughts concerning the problem. Try to see it from that viewpoint.

3. Explain your feelings as honestly and as calmly as you can. If your sexual code is different, say so. Do not pretend that you agree with the child's standards if you do not. On the other hand, you may agree and not be aware of it. Be sure that semantics are not keeping you from communicating.

4. Do not judge. Remember, *your* right and wrong need not be another's right and wrong. Your child is an individual. This is the most difficult point for a parent to grasp.

5. Try to help your child be responsible in making sexual decisions—to be aware of the consequence for the other party, for the family, for friends.

6. Talk on the level of what you feel to be the child's moral development, or at one level above. (Check yourself first to ascertain that you are not speaking from the lowest "obey me" level.)

7. Decide what action to take according to the child's age. Be sure to include him or her in the decision. And remember, you cannot *make* a child do anything.

If the Problem Is One of Integrity

1. Find out what motivated the child to act in this way.
2. Find out how the child feels about the action.
3. Express your feelings candidly and rationally.
4. Do not judge. Remember, peer pressure on your child may be stronger than yours. Any judgment you make can be from your frame of reference only.
5. Hold the child accountable for what was done. Do not let the blame be shifted.
6. If the school was involved (stealing, cheating, etc.), discuss the situation with the teacher and/or the principal and your child.
7. Work out together how the child will make reparation.
8. Once again, try to work at the child's moral stage, or one level above.
9. In dealing with small children, it is wise to remove causes of dishonesty where possible until they grow in moral strength. For instance, let a teacher proctor tests more carefully, or let a mother not leave money around to tempt a reaching hand.

If the Problem Is One of Unkindness to Classmates

1. Discuss the situation with your child as has been suggested—listen, elicit motivations and feelings, communicate your own feelings in response to the wrong behavior.
2. Discuss the situation with your child and the teacher. Ask for a description of the behavior from the teacher's viewpoint.
3. Help your child take responsibility for hurting others.
4. Figure out with your child how to make reparation.
5. Outline ways to avoid repeating the behavior. How can the child change? How can the situation change? What kind of help will be required?
6. Check to ascertain that you are attempting to work at the child's own level of moral development.

No guidelines serve to solve the problems parents have with their children, be they academic, behavioral, social, or moral. The child as an individual and the parent as an individual make each encounter unique. Dynamics can both solve and destroy. What guidelines do is keep parents from running away with themselves in their hurt and anger and frustration.

Only one rule holds fast for all parents at all times. They can make every mistake in the book, but only one is irreversible. That is the taking away of love.

Dear Mrs. Miller:

What is the best way for a parent to help a son with his homework?

Mrs. A.

Dear Mrs. A.:

The best way to help your son with his homework is to not *help him. Let me explain:*

1. Instead of answering his questions, steer him to places where he can find the answers himself—dictionary, encyclopedia, library, etc.

2. Instead of nagging him to do his homework, help him set up a work schedule. If he does not follow it, let him go to class unprepared. To make sure there will be consequences to bear, both of you should explain to the teacher the system you are following.

3. Don't sit with him while he does his work; *don't* check his work and correct the errors; *don't* do his work!

Homework is a means of letting both student and teacher know how and what a student is learning. Don't block the process.

Dear Mrs. Miller:

Our fifth-grade son is falling behind in his math. He says he works hard but just can't seem to understand and catch up with the class. We hate him to be getting F's all the time. What kind of help do you suggest?

The W.'s

Dear W's:

First, go with him to see the teacher, who may throw some light on the cause of the difficulty. If there is a learning problem, she will want to discuss it with you; if there is a behavior or no-homework problem, she will want to discuss that with him. If it is neither and he just doesn't get the math, ask whether she can give extra help to him in school. You might ask the teacher to lay out a program with which you, another family member, or even another student might help him. Short-term tutoring with a professional could see him over a temporary hurdle. One word of warning: don't let anyone do his work for him. Offer him guidance, not escape.

Dear Mrs. Miller:

My son did not do well in seventh grade this year. In fact, he was passed into eighth grade conditionally, and we are afraid he will be put back. Do you think we should send him to summer school?

B. L. N.

Dear B. L. N.:

Summer school may serve to reinforce the content of your son's seventh-grade courses or to introduce him to new courses he will take in the coming year. It probably won't, however, cure the problem that made him do poorly in the first place—unless it is a school specifically designed to meet his needs. What do his teachers say? Are his skills weak? One-to-one tutoring (either private or through a volunteer agency) may strengthen them. Is the work too difficult for him? Perhaps he needs a less demanding program. If the problem is that he does not apply himself to his studies, you have to look for reasons. Maybe he does not know how . . . maybe he is emotionally immature . . . maybe he is afraid to fail . . . maybe he is rebelling against parental pressures . . . maybe he has overextended himself in the activities. Talking with him and his teachers may give you answers to these questions. If not, ask his guidance counselor about an individualized evaluation of your son. Time and money spent on one now might forestall years of repeated failure at school. At any rate, don't expect summer school to turn him into a good student.

Dear Mrs. Miller:

What do you do with a kindergartener who won't go to school? He cries and screams every day. My husband and I are wrecks by nine o'clock.

J. and T. R.

Dear Mr. and Mrs. R.:

Leaving home for school is the first big trauma in your son's life. He is giving up his security—the place and the people that he feels at ease with. He is entering a new world with a stranger—his teacher. He has more rigid demands put upon him. And he is suddenly one child among many, instead of Mr. Special. Obviously, your son is afraid and, unable to deal with his feelings, he cries and screams. What to do? Try to keep calm. Reassure him constantly of your love for him—especially if there is a new baby in the house. Let him know you will be there when he comes home; if you work, let him know the same sitter will be there. However, be careful not to over-baby him. It is a fact that too much protection and too little both lead to insecurity. Walk the fine line.

Dear Mrs. Miller:

Jory, our son, is in kindergarten. He is the one parents and teachers complain about—the aggressive child. He hits and kicks and tears up the other children's toys. Nothing we do or his teacher does stops him. Please help.

L. and S. K.

Dear Mr. and Mrs. K.:
Aggressive behavior such as you describe is usually
an outward manifestation of stress within a child. Ana-
lyze Jory's situation and see if you can pinpoint and re-
lieve stress-causing factors. Is he overcompeting with sib-
lings? Does he feel he must strive to win your approval?
Has there been a recent change within the family—new
baby, death, divorce, a move? Does he see family fights?
How is his health? Is he small for his age? Is his diet sen-
sible and balanced? Does he have learning difficulties?
Take the pressure off any area where you see it. Ask
Jory's teacher to do the same. Talk with the school guid-
ance counselor or psychologist if his aggressiveness does
not lessen within a few months. Testing may be the way
to find the cause of his behavior.

Dear Mrs. Miller:
My fourth-grade son has been a disciplinary problem ever
since we moved into this new community a month ago. I
blame it on the schools. He was looking forward to the new
school—bright and eager. But the first day they gave him an
achievement test based on books he never had read. He did
poorly, and they put him back into third grade. Now he feels
like a failure. What can I do?

M. R.

Dear M. R.:
Postmortems are nonproductive, but I can't help
asking two questions. Why wasn't your son tested for
placement before the first day of school? Was your son a
disciplinary problem in his old school? With those an-
swered, the course of action is to turn around a destruc-
tive situation. Make an appointment for you, your hus-
band, and your son to seek help from the teacher and
person in charge of placement. Explain what is happen-
ing—how you and your husband feel, how you see your
son reacting. Let him explain how he feels. The school

*cannot know unless you tell them. Ask them to help you.
Do they want to give the boy extra help to move him up
a grade? Do they want to give him counseling to calm
him down? Can you and they encourage peer friendships
to give him a sense of belonging? How can you help
strengthen him to live through a painful reality? What
does the school suggest? Work with them to follow
through to a solution.*

Dear Mrs. Miller:

I am writing this letter for my neighbors, who are Greek
and don't speak very much English. They have a daughter
who is in the sixth grade in school. She speaks English, but
not so well, and she has a heavy accent. The kids in her class
make fun of her, and she comes home crying almost every day.
I feel so bad for her. What can we do?

P. F.

Dear P. F.:

*You are indeed a good neighbor and friend. I suggest
you set up a meeting with the teacher, the girl, and her
parents. You had better be there to interpret. Explain
the problem and the pain the girl is suffering. There are
many things the teacher could do to inform the class of
the rich Greek heritage from which America has borrowed: a trip to the museum; learning the Greek alphabet and finding current uses of it; cooking a Greek dish
for the class to sample; reading parts of the* Iliad *or Od-*
yssey; *a walking tour to look for signs of Greek architecture. Meanwhile, perhaps you could give the child some
speech lessons; maybe the teacher would even let a classmate do it. However, the main thing is for her to develop
pride in her culture and in herself to withstand taunts.
Greek or not, we are all subject to them during our lifetime.*

Dear Mrs. Miller:

Our son Albert, a freshman in high school, has been the butt of his class every year since first grade. Kids just don't like him. He is a sweet, gentle boy, but not well coordinated and not a great student. Still, he has a heart and suffers greatly. What can my husband and I do?

The A.'s

Dear Mr. and Mrs. A.:

Try to help Albert on two levels. One: work with him to find out what it is about him that children don't like. Can it be simply coordination and grades? Perhaps he has some bad habits he can rid himself of. You and he might talk with his teachers or guidance counselor. Talk with Albert about how he sees himself. Two: support him as a person in his own right—not one who exists only as others see him. If he is not acceptable to his classmates, the fault may lie with them, not with him. Help him learn to cope with them. A firm called Grothe Associates (P.O. Box 580, Lincoln, Maine 01773), puts out cassettes and booklets to help in this area. You might try them.

Dear Mrs. Miller:

We are planning a move to another community. Our seven-year-old is giving us a bad time about it since he is very close to the neighborhood children. How can I make the transition easier for him, and do you think it would be easier for a child of ten or eleven?

Mrs. H.

Dear Mrs. H.:

I think the child and the way the move is handled make more difference than his age. Upset is normal when a child leaves the friends and school and neighborhood where he feels comfortable. Like Columbus, he is embarking for a new world, and he is scared. The move will test his ego. He is leaving a place where he knows his

*role for the unknown, where he will have to prove himself
and find a new role. Let him know that you understand
his fears, that you have some of your own in facing a
similar situation. But help him see the experience as a
challenge to himself and to the family . . . as an opening
of new doors. Be sure to take along addresses so that he
can correspond with friends and a favorite teacher. If it
is feasible, plan a return visit. In the new home, be pa-
tient. His insecurity may express itself as hostility. Encourage, but don't push, new friendships. Relax—he will
have "best friends" before you do!*

Dear Mrs. Miller:

My eleventh-grade daughter takes a required course in
Family Living. They have discussed things like dating and sex,
marriage and children, which is O.K. But now they are going
to be talking about abortion, which my husband and I strongly
disapprove of. The school won't leave the subject out of the
course, but can we refuse to have our daughter go to class?

Mrs. G. D.

Dear Mrs. D.:

*Legally, in most states, you as parents have the right
to forbid your child to discuss or read anything which
goes against your family's values or beliefs. However, I
urge you to let your daughter continue in the Family
Living class, despite your disapproval of abortion. She is
almost an adult. If she has facts with which to form an
opinion, she will be more likely to make that opinion a
responsible one—more so than if she formed her opinion
merely on your beliefs. Bring the subject up at home.
Certainly, your values, which have already played an important part in her growth, will continue to play a strong
role in helping her reach a decision. Don't fear different
views on any subject. Hiding them from children only
makes them more intriguing. Facing them puts them in
proper persepctive.*

Dear Mrs. Miller:

Are there any programs for teaching elementary school children morals? If that sounds too Victorian, call it ethics or values. Do you know of any such programs I could use?

Teacher Who Sees a Need

Dear Teacher:

Seeing the need puts you halfway there. Congratulations! Yes, there are programs. Some textbook publishers have books available. Other people offer supportive guidelines. I suggest you write to the following people: Ms. Katherine Sanders, The Quality Educators Ltd., 1236 Southeast 4th Avenue, Fort Lauderdale, Florida 33316; Professor Sidney Simon, University of Massachusetts, Amherst, Massachusetts 01002; Dr. Lawrence Kohlberg, Harvard Center for Moral Education, Cambridge, Massachusetts 02138; The American Bar Association, 36 West 44th Street, New York, New York 10036.

All of the foregoing share your concern over the need for moral (and, in the case of the Bar Association, legal) education. Since each approaches it in a different way, ask for materials from all of them. Then put together a program combining the information that best suits the needs of your students. You will have better luck if you involve their parents too: morals are a shared job.

Dear Mrs. Miller:

The kids in my class (I am a junior in high school) cheat an awful lot. They take answers into tests and copy each other's papers. They plagiarize like crazy on term papers. I play it straight and don't get such great marks, which makes me mad. Do you think I should tell the teachers what's going on?

A Female Student

Dear Student:

Consider yourself fortunate to have the values and the independence to avoid the cheating which is preva-

lent in many schools and colleges. Long after marks are forgotten, you will have the character and sense of reality to sustain you through the tough moments of life. Your classmates will find themselves floundering and looking for other fantasy solutions to their problems. But that probably doesn't help you much now. Of course you are mad. As for telling—that is a decision, a hard one, you have to make. The teachers must suspect something already and probably want to avoid the issue; it sounds as if it would be difficult not to be aware. You may or may not stir them to take action. You may come off as a goody-goody—or as a crusader. Ponder the variables and then make your decision, aware of the possible outcomes. Whatever you decide, be sure that your personal commitment to honesty is right.

Dear Mrs. Miller:

Our eleventh-grader is taking a course called "My Values." It teaches the kids about sex and religion and things that my husband and I think do not belong in a classroom. We think the home is where you teach a kid right from wrong. We are not fighting the school on it, but we would like your opinion. Are we being old-fashioned?

Mr. and Mrs. M. T.

Dear Mr. and Mrs. T.:

I think you are being unrealistic rather than old-fashioned. Remember, you are not asked to abdicate your responsibility just because the school is teaching values—it is a job for both of you. Young people form their values through example and experience, which take place all their waking hours, wherever they are. This kind of learning cannot be relegated to non-school hours when they are home with their parents. That would be like insisting your child read only when in school, since that is where reading is learned. Relationships in school, competition, decision-making on tests, homework, sports,

*friends, behavior—all these help form your child's sense
of values. It is a wise school that takes advantage of
them. It is a wise parent that supplements them.*

Dear Mrs. Miller:
 I found a contraceptive in my fifteen-year-old son's wallet.
If I tell my husband, he'll kill him. What should I do.
                                                    Mrs. G.

Dear Mrs. G.:
 *If you were snooping in your son's wallet, the first
thing you should do is apologize. It will be hard for him
to trust you in a discussion of sex if he feels you don't
trust him enough to respect his privacy. But try anyway.
Maybe he carries the contraceptive as a symbol of the
manhood he is close to achieving. Maybe he is actually
using it as protection in a sexual relationship. In the former case, try to understand; in the latter, be grateful he
is not having the relationship without protection.*
 *I think you and your husband and son are probably
due for an honest discussion of adolescent sexual feelings
and needs. Don't preach, but be sure to point out the
emotional responsibility that a sexual relationship entails.*

7/Something Old,
Something New—
in Education

Holly Watson is a junior in high school. At the start of the year she and her classmates had a large voice in determining what courses she would take. She carries six courses, but one meets only once a week since she is working independently; another meets twice a week for three hours at a stretch. Some days she has only one scheduled class and spends the rest of her time working alone on an individualized program. Mrs. Watson says, "Call it what you will, this is what education should be. I wish I'd had it when I was a kid."

Peter Hoffman is also a junior in high school. He carries four major subjects—English, Intermediate Algebra, American History, and French—and an art elective. In order to accommodate a full school schedule, all of his classes meet four days a week for fifty minutes. He spends several hours a day on homework, takes good notes in class, participates in discussions, passes weekly quizzes, quarterly tests, and semester exams. He writes term papers. Mr. and Mrs. Hoffman are pleased. "Peter's getting a good solid education," they say. "No fluffs and frills. He studies hard and he is learning. What more can you ask of a school?"

Actually, Holly and Peter are in the same school system—Scarsdale, New York. Only Peter attends traditional Scarsdale High, and Holly has opted for the newer Alternate School. They attended the same elementary school, then went their separate ways. Oriented toward academic achievement, Peter's parents steered him to one of the regular junior highs, where he was prepared to meet the demands of the competitive college preparatory course at Scarsdale High. The Watsons, on the other hand, feared that the inflexibility of traditional education might stifle Holly's natural curiosity. They put her in Choice, Scarsdale's alternate junior high.

Students in both alternate schools are accepted only after an examination of their past records. "We don't want the school to be known as a dumping ground for behavior problems who can't make it in the regular school," the staff says. Choice and Alternate School are for the self-motivated, the inventive, the curious who want to share in control of their education. The programs are created to give them enough room to create their own learning experiences and, at the same time, enough guidance to hold them accountable for achievement.

Scarsdale's traditional junior high and high schools are highly rated by both parents and educators. A combination of strong basics plus electives challenges the able student like Peter while at the same time offering reinforcement to weaker students. There are programs for both college- and noncollege-bound students, in a setting that looks familiar to the parents and grandparents of the students who attend.

The Watsons and the Hoffmans are lucky; their community provides equally good parallel systems of education so that both may choose the kind of school they feel is best equipped to help their child learn. If every school district in the country were able to do the same, our educational system might avoid its present excoriation.

When parents are happy with their children's learning, they tend to become disciples of their school philosophy; thus the Watsons advocate open education; while the Hoffmans favor the traditional system. Neither might be able to argue their case on educational grounds or statistics. They have a stronger argument: experience.

Both sets of parents see things taking place in their children that make them feel good. The children are happy; they enjoy school, and they are doing well. Peter's report card is filled with A's and B's. Holly receives positive comment slips from her teachers. Their teachers care. The principal of each school is readily available. Parents are active and involved. Discipline is a minor problem.

Had Peter been unsuccessful at Scarsdale High and Holly unhappy in Alternate School, both sets of parents might have felt differently. Displeased and resentful, they could have become critics instead of advocates.

While experience is one of the most valid bases for forming an opinion, it leaves itself open to misinterpretation. Some parents who have a positive experience with children in school are not satisfied simply to support the kind of education their school offers; they go further and denounce any other. They oversimplify, like the third-grader whose teacher praised one of her two drawings. "What's wrong with the other?" the child asked, hurt. Nothing has to be wrong with the other simply because parents are satisfied with either an open or a traditional school.

In addition to personal experience, parents tend to assess schools in two other ways. One is by hearsay. Parents listen to each other, and school is a constant topic of their conversation, especially when attitudes are critical. Any teacher knows that one of the worst enemies is a network of gossiping parents, who can distort facts the way a fun house mirror does an image. Faced with a real—or imagined—problem in school, parents are quick to blame a teacher or classmate rather than their own child.

Open education has been an easy scapegoat for such parents: "Johnny doesn't read because all he ever does in school is play games." Traditional education can be an easy scapegoat too: "Jane gets bad marks because the teacher doesn't give her individual attention." In both cases, to secure reinforcement the parents spread the word to other parents who, like them, overreact. In these highly charged communications, facts play little part.

The other way parents assess schools is by lining them up alongside their own expectations. In Hanover, New Hampshire, a high percentage of parents are associated with Dartmouth College; their educational demands include strong academics, leading to high SAT scores and acceptance in the top competitive colleges. While they do not shrug off the value of self-motivation, they do not want to take a chance. They insist on traditional schools.

John Dewey High School in New York, on the other hand, attracts parents who are more interested in the learning process than in the material learned. Their children also acquire skills and get good SAT scores and are admitted to the colleges of their choice, but through a different route. These parents support student self-determination and individualization. They want an open school.

As you look across the country, you see many primary and elementary schools that have abandoned traditional classrooms in favor of open ones. Yet you see few high schools offering open education. One of the reasons for this is also parental expectations. In the lower grades parents are willing to risk innovation that claims to build self-confidence and inner resources—especially if it keeps their children happy. They can reassure themselves by saying, "If it doesn't work, and my child fails to learn arithmetic this year, next year will be time enough."

In high school, however, next year holds dangers: the student has to get into college. This requires good marks and a high class rank, along with SAT's as close to 800 as possible to impress the Director of Admissions. Therefore, parents fall back on a sure thing—the way it worked for them.

One of the most dramatic examples I have ever seen of this shift in parental expectation is in Utah. Howell has a one-room schoolhouse covering kindergarten through grade six. Kate Dennis, who not only is head teacher there but also almost single-handedly developed the entire program, runs a totally open school. Each child meets with Kate weekly to set up an individualized program. Following the progress of each, she works individually and in small groups and has children work with one another. From the five-year-old "reading" her book to the eleven-year-old with math sets, students are independent, involved, and happy. It is easy to see why the parents of Howell Elementary School consider themselves the most fortunate in the world.

The high schools these children attend later on are so different as to be another world. Parents accept this because in fact they see high school as another world—one in which their children's "success" will lead to college acceptance. Courses are prescribed and taught in large, desk-lined classrooms, using standard textbooks. Competition is strong—not only in academic achievement but in sports, band, and cheerleading. The atmosphere is restrictive. As the principal says with pride, "We have no behavior problems here." According to the young people with whom I spoke, there are very few happy students either.

While parents think their educational hopes for their particular children are unique, most parents want school to accomplish the same thing in general terms: to prepare their children for life. It is the differences in interpreting what is meant by "life" that form the basis for arguments about the various forms of education.

As you read through the following list, try making a check mark next to each statement with which you agree, completing the sentence: I want my child as an adult to be able . . .

1. To enjoy life.
2. To reach his or her full potential.
3. To think.
4. To love.
5. To contribute to the community.
6. To have a good self-image.
7. To make decisions independently.
8. To have values and stand up for them.
9. To do meaningful work.
10. To be self-supporting.

If you are like most parents, you have checked every one of the ten statements—no matter what kind of education you support. Modernists and traditionalists have more in common than they imagine, but they have been too busy arguing to realize it. They do not want different things for their children; they merely approach the achievement of them in different ways.

As far back as the fourth century B.C., Aristotle proposed a kind of open education when he said, "Teaching is not teaching a student to see, but providing an experience so that students discover they *can* see." Our Puritan forebears, however, saw education in a basic mold: "Teach children," they said, "to read and understand the principles of religion and the capital laws of the country."

Until the mid-1800s, American schools followed the elitist pattern of their British models, providing a broad classical education to the chosen few. But with the Industrial Revolution, education was recognized as a right for the masses, and elitism gave way to populism, bringing with it rigid, standardized methods and courses.

With education compulsory, no one gave much thought to its quality until philosopher and educator John Dewey came along in the early 1900s and hurled a challenge. "We need not teach a child *what* to think, but *how* to think," he wrote, echoing Aristotle twenty-four centuries earlier.

Then in 1957 Russia sent up Sputnik, and our immediate reaction was, "Their schools must be better than ours!" With John Dewey only five years dead, we threw out his ideas of progressive education. Traditional education became even more traditional in our efforts to beat the Russians.

However, society never stands still. The 1960s Civil Rights movement brought open education back into America's schools as a means of providing individualized instruction to meet minority needs. Taking as their model the open classroom so successful in Britain's Leicestershire Integrated Day and other infant schools, such leading American educators, writers, and intellectuals as John Holt, Jonathan Kozol, Paul Goodman, Herbert Kohl, and Edgar Friedenberg proposed various adaptations of these new methods to America's needs. Open education was the rage for a while until juvenile crime ran rampant, test scores continued to decline, truancy got out of hand, and Americans cried again for a change. "Back to Basics" was reborn.

This time, though, the open classrooms were not obliterated. Instead, the two different educational approaches now stand in face-to-face conflict. As in a tug-of-war, parents align themselves behind a leader and pull. While parents on both sides of the rope have strong *feelings*, their *understanding* is weak.

DIFFERENCES BETWEEN BASIC AND OPEN EDUCATION

Open education is centered on children learning; in traditional education the focus is on teachers teaching. The Council for Basic Education, which foreshadowed Back to Basics in the 1950s, supports traditional schools because they "stress academic achievement in teacher-centered classrooms." Jean Piaget, psychologist and educator, on the other hand, advocates the discovery approach of open schools because "to understand something, the child must invent or rediscover it for himself." In these divergent viewpoints lie the main philosophical differences between the two educational approaches.

Traditional education presupposes that the teacher has the answer, and must make students work before giving it to them, motivating them, amusing them, stimulating them, and holding their interest. Through lectures, assigned reading, discussion, and drill, the teacher prepares students to understand and to be able to use the information given. A good teacher serves as a role model as well as a mark giver to urge students to work to their full potential.

Open education assumes that the answer lies within each child. Children search to find it, and the teacher understands what they are searching for and guides them in their discovery. Curiosity, fun, the excitement of discovery provide the motivation to learn.

In the former kind of education, the teacher sets up evaluative criteria to let children know whether they have gotten the answer, how close they have come, or whether they have failed completely. The criteria are determined by tests created around what the teacher wants the child to learn in the time the teacher deems reasonable. As the Council for Basic Education says, basic education is teacher-centered.

In open education, however, children and teachers together set up their evaluative criteria. They decide to learn a certain skill or to work through a problem important to them. When they have mastered the skill or solved the problem, they have learned. There is no time limit and no comparison with other students. They learn as individuals what they are ready to learn. They evaluate themselves as they go along. They do not come close to learning, and they do not fail. They continue until they succeed on their own terms.

It is, therefore, achievement that matters in traditional education, while it is the process of learning that matters in open education.

The role of the teacher also differs sharply in the two kinds of education. In the traditional classroom, the teacher is boss: knowing the material, providing the material, evaluating the results. The student decides only whether or not to work as directed. In open schools, the teacher shares authority with the student. The teacher provides a stimulating environment to spark the student's curiosity. The student pursues interests as determined under the teacher's guidance when guidance is needed, alone when confident. Student and teacher together create the learning experience, and together they evaluate it.

"No teacher can be a fountain of knowledge any more," writes Lola May, Mathematics Consultant, in *PTA Magazine.* "We can't find students who will sit long enough to be sponges either. We know now that the role of the teacher is to be a guide." As a guide in this new role, the teacher learns as well as teaches; as a decision-maker, also a new role, the student also teaches.

In the last analysis, the greatest philosophical difference between these two forms of education is in their views of children. Assuming the sameness of children, basic education groups them together by age and teaches them the same lessons. Open schools, considering each child unique, individualize instruction according to the interests and readiness of every pupil.

In basic schools, children deviate from the norm as they perform better or less well than the average. On a Bell curve, they get their A's and F's at either end of the C's, being labeled "bright," "slow," or "average." In open schools, there is no norm, for each child performs independently. A nine-year-old reading at second-grade level is not considered a slow fourth-grader, as in basic schools, but simply a nine-year-old reading. Grade levels are too arbitrary for open schools; reading levels are too standardized. In over half the nation's open schools, personalized comments are used instead of grades. When grades are used, however, they are based solely on the student's work, not on a comparative curve.

"What about Back to Basics?" some parents may ask. "Isn't that the real difference between the two kinds of schools?"

No. Good schools, be they old or new, have always taught basics. And bad schools, whatever their methods, have not. The difference lies in the emphasis they put on basics. Traditional schools consider mastery of the required material the goal toward which they strive. Open schools encourage students to create their own material. Basic schools drill in skills and outlined curriculums. Open schools eliminate drill, motivating students to acquire skills and information through their own interests. For instance, in order to pursue an interest in butterflies, a child must know how to read, perhaps even improve reading skills to read the more informative books.

The very definition of the word "basics" may differ between the two kinds of schools as well. Traditional schools cling to the three-Rs concept, while open schools go much further. Willy Black, 1979 National Teacher of the Year, defines the basics as "reading, writing, listening, reflecting, and creating."

She adds, "I would like to see a basic that every child be given a variety of activities so that he can gain a good self-image ... The basics mean being able to meet a problem head-on ... having enough interests and skills to make a worthy use of one's leisure time ... feeling responsible for one's fellow man. The basics mean a nurturing of the inner spirit that makes some people great and encourages all to move forth and create."

Structure

A traditional classroom looks different from an open classroom. Whereas, in the former room, the teacher's desk dominates rows of student desks, in the latter, the teacher's desk is not visible. There may not even be one.

A traditional classroom looks neat. Many a principal takes pride in the neatness of the school, sending sharp notes to errant teachers who leave papers and books around. Student's texts and work materials are to be kept in their desks or cubbyholes. Books are to be stacked on shelves, and audiovisual equipment stands in the corner out of the way. A lively elementary classroom will have walls covered with student paintings and compositions, along with pictures the teacher has posted to coordinate with lessons. Many have caged animals, such as hamsters, to aid the teacher in the dual lessons of responsibility and reproduction.

An open classroom, on the other hand, may look messy by comparison, for neatness as such is not demanded by the openschool principal. In the lower grades *things* are everywhere to stimulate interest and pique the curiosity of little learners. Every flat surface is filled with books, games, files, source materials, caged animals, etc. Walls are equally cluttered. From the ceiling hang signs, exhibits, mobiles. On the floor lie rugs, cushions, and spread-out children. Among them all may be the teacher, sitting cross-legged with a small group learning long division and often difficult to locate.

In traditional classrooms students are to be found in their seats unless one is talking with the teacher or giving a report at the front. In an open classroom a child may be anywhere. In Sue Talbot's first grade in Indiana, a child may be reading alone in a miniature railroad car; in Dolores Keller's fifth grade in Florida, in a "thinking" tent. A student may be building a life-size papier-maché horse in New Hampshire or working in the hallway in Westchester or climbing to a loft in Colorado. For while traditional classrooms are designed to meet the needs of *all,* open classrooms are designed to meet the needs of *each.* All the former look alike; each of the latter looks different.

Time structure is looser in open schools as well. While all run their day by the clock to some degree, open classrooms are flexible enough to abandon schedules when student interest leads in unexpected directions. This is far less true in traditional schools. In most of them at elementary, junior high, and high school levels, class ends when the bell rings. The teacher has lesson plans, filed with the supervisor each week, that must be followed. Only by adhering rigidly to the bell schedule can each teacher be assured of doing that.

Not forced to follow a set time schedule, students in open

schools are rarely blocked from completing a study unit they have undertaken. What they miss one day, they can make up another; the important thing is the satisfaction of continuity. Nor are they forbidden by schedules to pursue any subject that interests them; they don't even have to do it within the confines of the school. Yet each year in traditional schools thousands of students are unable to take a course the way they want, thousands of teachers are deprived of eager students "because it doesn't fit the schedule."

Although both types of classrooms have a standard curriculum imposed from the outside (either the school district, Board of Education, or the state education department) that determines what should be studied at each grade level, the open classroom allows greater freedom in presenting that curriculum. Ideally, the subject matter evolves from the teacher-student dynamic itself. Of course, basic skills are covered in small-group teachings, but practice occurs unconventionally. For instance, while one child studies photography and another hamsters, each will learn reading in order to further pursue these interests: one to learn how to take pictures, the other to learn about breeding animals. Each will learn math, but again through different routes: one will measure solutions for developing negatives; the other will construct cages.

Some years ago in Newton, Massachusetts, the Murray Road High School experimented with the ultimate in open education. When students and teachers appeared in the fall, no classes were listed, no schedules handed out. They spent the first three weeks creating them together: students and teachers posted on a bulletin board courses they would like to take and give, respectively. By mixing, matching, and compromising, they devised a course of study and a schedule that met everyone's needs. Work was highly individualized, and teachers often met with students at night, before breakfast, or on weekends to free them for meetings with other teachers at more conventional hours. Although the school no longer exists, many teachers and students remember it as the most fulfilling educational experience of their lives.

In discussing structure, one cannot ignore the architectural design of the two kinds of schools. Open-school learning areas should radiate from a central media center, which is the heart of the school. There should be few walls but, rather, movable partitions that allow for flexible groupings. Traditional schools are designed more like egg cartons, each classroom isolated from others with walls and doors. The assembly hall and library are larger egg sections, unconnected to the whole. Noise in the halls and visitors are closed out of traditional classrooms as disturbing elements. But because of the constant flow in an open school, noise and visitors are not obtrusive, so there is no attempt to close them out.

Since ideal conditions rarely exist, open-classroom teachers often find themselves adapting to traditional schools, and traditional teachers to open schools. Hazelwood East High School in St. Louis saw both going on simultaneously. Built in 1975 as an open school, Hazelwood East had no classrooms per se—merely large, brightly colored partitions that could be shifted on tracks to form work areas. The teachers were all volunteers from the district's traditional high school.

Two years later, community pressure forced the school to abandon open teaching and revert to traditional. The panels were rolled around to enclose "classrooms" as fully as possible, although they still remained open to the corridor. Desks were aligned in rows with the teacher's up front. A traditional curriculum accompanied the structural changes, and the faculty adapted traditional teaching to an open school.

All but one. An English teacher named Beverly Bimes was so committed to her teaching philosophy that she could not abandon it. Although her room was made to look like the others and her desks were arranged in similar rows, she kept her teaching open. By seating students in a circle during class and returning them to rows at the end, by opening panels to pull her neighbor's class into a team-teaching situation once a day and closing them after class, Beverly Bimes was able to adapt open teaching to what had become a closed structure. She adapted it so well that school administrators noted outstanding achievement among her pupils, both in high school and later on in college. So successful have her teaching methods been that from among all the nation's teachers, she was selected National Teacher of the Year for 1980.

Materials

In standard traditional schools, the materials used—that is, those things through which education is imparted—are notebooks, textbooks, blue books, and books borrowed from the library for source papers. How much further a teacher goes beyond this depends on individual inventiveness rather than on the demands of traditional teaching. In open schools the materials are more varied: books, of course, line the classroom walls, homemade games teach spelling and numbers, rag dolls representing different professions, and masks, science experiments, birds' nests and dried milkweed, microscopes, scales, and homemade cake abound. There are hundreds of individualized lessons the teacher creates and duplicates for students. There are boxes of suggested things to do, whether a child likes dogs, dolls, or dinosaurs.

Both kinds of schools use audiovisual aids, but they use them differently. In traditional schools, the children are shown slides, movies, and videotapes. Students in open schools participate more actively. Instead of listening and watching, they make tapes, they take their own tests on cassettes, they hook themselves up to teaching programs, they make films and instruct each other with them. New York's John Dewey High School is said to have more teaching aids to augment its individualized program than most standard high schools in any chosen district have all together.

It is interesting to note that our greatest technological advance, the computer, has brought open-classroom techniques to even the most traditional schools. For a computer and a student can work only on a one-to-one relationship. Teachers can *explain* how the computer works, but a student must *experience* it alone. And experiencing is what open education is all about.

EVALUATING THE TWO SYSTEMS

No system of education is perfect. Most educators realize that whatever system is currently in use is falling short of the job to some degree. They are disheartened when, no matter what their method or philosophy, they come under general attack. It is strange, then, that they have not educated themselves to an awareness that neither the traditional nor the open school alone can solve their problems.

The few schools that come close to attaining excellence combine elements of each. But that too poses problems. Some parents favoring the traditional approach object to the liberal elements, while others on the side of open education object to the conservative elements. What is needed, clearly, is a better understanding of the strengths and weaknesses of the two approaches so that the best of both can be utilized.

Strengths of Traditional Education

First of all, traditional teaching is less unsettling than open teaching to students and parents, most of whom have been raised on it. They are familiar with the ground rules: work hard and do what your teacher says. Suddenly thrust into an open school, students tend to feel lost; they may miss the conventional structure and guidelines. As a result, their parents react negatively. And, as I have stated repeatedly, when parents pull against the school, it is all but impossible for a child to have a positive learning experience.

Second, it is easier to find trained teachers for traditional schools. Traditional teaching puts less of a demand on a teacher's personal qualities than open teaching does. The qualities a teacher needs can be honed at a good school of education, such as Harvard or the University of Massachusetts: organization, knowledge of subject, follow-through, patience, understanding of young people, personal relations, etc. Not every man or woman can be a good teacher; given someone who can and wants to be, a good college can train that person to do the job well in a traditional setting.

Third, traditional education meshes better with union rules and regulations. Teacher unions today are important forces in educational systems. They determine when and how long a teacher can teach, as a New York City teacher learned when the United Federation of Teachers prohibited her from giving extra help to a student after school. The preset hours and curriculums of traditional schools put fewer demands for extra hours or varying schedules on a teacher, making it easier to stay on good terms with the union.

Finally, traditional methods make it easier to communicate with parents about a student's performance. Marks and standardized report-card forms enable teachers to let parents know quickly and easily how their children are doing. When these are accompanied by thoughtful comments, parents can, with little effort, be kept informed of each child's progress.

Strengths of Open Education

Children in open classrooms enjoy school more. Statistics show a far lower truancy rate in open schools—even in those set up in deprived areas to handle so-called incorrigibles. This stands to reason: children who are involved are turned on; children having to obey are turned off.

The teachers enjoy school more. Even teachers who originally had to be coerced into open teaching have come around to admitting that it's much more exciting. Like the children, they are able to create instead of follow, designing both curriculum and teaching methods. In addition, they find themselves having to discipline very little: happy children are good children.

Finally, it equips children to cope better with life. Although no one has yet followed pupils of open schools into adult life, the indications are that they are building the qualities that lead to fulfilled living. For instance, according to many parents, they are less dependent on television, being more involved in projects carried over from school, and are better able to cope with problems that arise. Many junior high school teachers notice that children from open classrooms approach their work more maturely, requiring less outside pressure, that they are less competitive, more able to cooperate with a group. Open high schools, used as alternatives to traditional schools for difficult boys and girls, have found that behavior problems all but disappear. Transposing these qualities to adulthood, one can only believe that such children will face life more capably than many of us who were products of traditional learning.

Drawbacks of Traditional Education

First, the traditional classroom tends to be boring. Certainly there are eager students who learn in traditional schools with great enthusiasm. However, the majority are bored, tuned out and turned off. Millions of kids staring out of windows or cutting class or dropping out of school testify to that. When students are uninvolved, they are uninterested.

Moreover, there is too much pressure. Traditional education makes a child *have* to succeed. A child who conforms to the demands of the teacher is "good"; one who deviates is "bad." Since these labels extend into the home, pressure to succeed, to be what others want you to be, never eases. Failure carries a stigma in traditional schools, indicating what a student did not or could not do. To live under the pressure of impending failure daily is more than most adults could survive.

It also relies on outside controls. Although America is the "home of the free," its traditional education does little to train young people to use their freedom wisely. Throughout their school years, children are controlled by outside forces—school rules, bells, schedules, proctored exams, orders from a teacher. They are taught to obey, not to control themselves. Therefore, when the controls are removed—in high school, in college, in adult life—young people often fall apart. The drop-out rates in all three areas indicate inability to cope. If schools were able to build inner controls, there might be less dropping out.

Drawbacks of Open Education

It is important to note that not all children can handle open education and that certain of them fare poorly in an open classroom. The child geared to learn through hearing rather than through seeing will not do well where the bulk of teaching is visual. The child whose parents are critical of open education is likely to reflect their negative attitude. The rigid child, used to assignments and schedules, will have trouble at first. The insecure child, afraid to attempt the new, may withdraw under the responsibility of free choice. And the child whose imagination has been stifled is likely to feel lost.

Another problem is the difficulty in getting good teachers, since so few schools of education prepare teachers for open classrooms. Usually, the school hiring them must do its own training. Many teachers graduating from college have never been exposed to an open classroom, much less been given the skills of teaching there. As a result, many open classrooms have inadequate teachers, turning open teaching into open chaos. Instead of guiding, they turn students loose; instead of individualizing, they lose track. It is little wonder that some parents have run back to basics when they have seen open classrooms so ill managed.

ALTERNATIVE EDUCATIONAL PROGRAMS

The recently retired Commissioner of Education, Ernest Boyer, stated, "Schools in America must be encouraged to develop a variety of alternative approaches to meet different needs." He realized that mass education cannot work as it once did. As Dr. Boyer pointed out, "The school is the only institution in America where we take the entire population and assume that everyone will perform in the same way for an extended period of time."

Today throughout the country there are tens of thousands of alternative schools responding to the individual needs of children. It is helpful to parents to know what alternatives are available—perhaps in their school; if not, in their district. If none is offered where you live, you can urge your local superintendent of schools or board of education to institute them. If the board fails to respond, you can use your own initiative to try to establish a separate alternative school within the community. Many private foundations are interested in such pilot programs. Even the government's National Institute of Education has a Model Schools Program with funds expressly for this purpose. Some of the alternatives already existing in schools across the country follow.

Outdoor Education

This is an attempt to bring children in closer contact with their environment. A class is taken for a week into an outdoor education area—such as a state or county park or a wildlife conservation area. Regular school studies are abandoned, and students are taught by environmental specialists to obtain an understanding of nature and the environment. In the process they use skills they have learned in school—reading, math, art—and apply them to their outdoor studies. On returning to the classroom, the regular teachers who have accompanied the children follow through on the lessons of environmental education.

The aim: To reintroduce children to their heritage in nature, making them more environmentally aware and responsible.

Work-Study Program

Many schools give credit for work done outside the school, either on a paid or volunteer basis. One girl spent two afternoons a week at a local broadcasting station. Another worked with deaf children. One school gave a boy a semester off to become part of a political campaign. Another gave credit for a summer spent working in urban renewal. Many schools devote a three-week midwinter period to out-of-school activities in which students put on plays, travel, work in hospitals, do scientific experiments, or read to the blind. Work-study programs enable students to see education in a framework larger than the school and to see its value as broader than the marks on a report card. It also enables the nonacademic student to find areas in which to excel.

The aim: To integrate the skills of school with the skills of life.

Bilingual Education

Bilingual education expanded in 1971 to deal with the needs of Puerto Rican children in New York City. Speaking only Spanish, these students lost Dick and Jane along with the ability to read anything else and understand what their teacher said. Spanish-speaking classes were instituted for them as a transition into their new English-speaking world. Similar programs have been introduced in other parts of the country where two languages are prevalent: in San Francisco with Chinese; in New York with Haitian French; in Florida, Colorado, and California with Spanish. In all, the United States Department of Education sponsors almost seven hundred bilingual projects. An interesting switch is that many English-speaking parents have enrolled their children in bilingual classes as a way of having them grow up with a second language.

The aim: Better communications and recognition of minorities within the community.

Bicultural Education

The phrase "Black is beautiful" brought bicultural education to our schools and colleges. When the black minority made the nation aware of its rich culture and contributions, Black Studies became a part of many curriculums. It swept the country with such impact that even white children began wearing Afro haircuts and caftans. Without knowing it, we became bicultural. More recently, as other minority groups have demanded recognition, programs of different cultures have appeared, among them—Italian, Cuban, Vietnamese, Mexican, and Chinese. Often they are integrated with a bilingual program, but not always. The most widespread minority culture to enter the schools is feminism, originating in the Women's Movement.

The aim: To enrich children's lives through understanding and appreciation of their own and one another's cultures.

Year-Round Schools

People have always deplored the summer hiatus in the school year, with school buildings standing idle, deteriorating in disuse, becoming subject to vandalism. Teachers frantically search for summer jobs in order to keep busy and to supplement their incomes. Children grow bored; the juvenile crime rate goes up. The year-round school developed in response to these and other concerns. The plan works two ways. One divides the school year into four quarters, offering families a choice of any three in which to send their children to school; teachers have the option of teaching three or four quarters. The other plan divides the school year into alternating periods, six weeks of school and then three of vacation. Parent advocates of year-round schools feel that they sustain learning; critics object to the disruption of family life-style. Teachers by and large approve but find the mechanics awkward. Students, of course, miss their long summer vacation.

The aim: To make better use of the school year.

Magnet Schools

A magnet school is actually another name for an alternative school of any kind. It offers a specific kind of education, getting its name from the fact that children will be drawn to it. These may be entire schools or self-contained units within larger schools, which are known as *mini-schools*. For years there have been magnet schools by other names—the School of Performing Arts, High School of Science, School of Art and Design. These admitted students selectively by testing. Many of today's magnet schools have open admissions, accepting any student who wants what they offer: art, oceanography, languages, open education, basic education, and so on.

The aim: To offer alternative ways of meeting the varying needs and interests of children.

Intensive Programming

Educators have debated for years the value of having children study five subjects simultaneously. Can students learn to capacity when they have to turn off a subject at the ringing of a bell? Can children's minds carry five separate disciplines all at once? Is there another way? Those educators answering "no" to the first two questions created intensive programming as an answer to the third. In this system a student is offered one subject only for a seven-week period, studying it throughout the day from different viewpoints. For instance, an intensive study of French would include French language, history, art and music, literature, science, and mathematics. At the end of seven weeks, the student would go on to another subject in the same way. Vacations are built into the school year as they are in other schools.

The aim: To let students learn in depth without compartmentalization.

Contract Teaching

Individualized teaching, as we have seen, puts responsibility for learning on the student. Contract teaching is a way the teacher and a student decide what material is to be covered in a certain period of time. They draw up a contract together at the start of the week, with the goal clearly defined. During the week the student works toward that goal, seeking help from the teacher when necessary. On attaining the goal, the student is ready to draw up another contract with the teacher. If the goal is not attained, however, the student has to continue working toward it, being penalized by giving up free periods or forfeiting play time. Children with less control may work on a daily contract, while more mature ones may draw up contracts for several weeks at a time.

The aim: To help children develop self-motivation and self-control in learning and in living.

Fundamental Schools

In the early 1970s, in reaction against open education, groups of parents clamored for alternatives in the form of basic schools. School systems obliged, opening either fundamental schools for their children or fundamental units within existing schools. All of them stress basic subjects, having abandoned the "frill" courses that open schools use in developing the total child. All of them emphasize reading scores, writing, grammar, and math, offering in addition the usual traditional curriculum. Many of them have moved toward reinstating dress codes and rigid discipline in a belief that when a child's body is regulated, the mind follows suit. To date, there are alternative fundamental schools in at least twenty states, with more springing up yearly.

The aim: To give children a strong academic program in a disciplined environment.

Individual Teaching Approaches

There are as many individual ways to teach as there are creative teachers in the country. While they cannot all be listed here, parents should be aware of the many different and wonderful kinds of teaching happening in classrooms. For instance, in Vermont Paul Kaplan taught his fifth grade through cross-country skiing: "For English, the vocabulary that skiing introduces; for science, what nature provides in the woods; for math, Celsius temperature scales and how to convert metric measures of ski equipment." In Colorado Mike Sipes taught his junior high kids during a trip down the Grand Canyon. Some schools use team teaching, with a group of teachers presenting materials together. Other schools combine subjects, so that English and history may be taught as one course, or art and music, or math and science. Many schools use students to teach each other, finding that the "learner" relates well to someone of the same age and that the "teacher" gains self-confidence. Most schools offer some kind of human relations program—sex education or marriage and the family or an investigation of personal values. Many schools offer courses in chess and bridge and computer games, as well as film and photography. Parents need not fear these innovations: they do not replace basics; they supplement them.

The aim: To reach children creatively in ways that stimulate their growth in all dimensions.

Despite the variety that the American school system offers families, it seems unable to fulfill the hopes of most of them. Resigned tolerance, complaints, or out-and-out fights seem to be the most frequent response to education today. It's high time that parents and educators drop the labels with which they tag schools. Education is not an either-or situation; people need not choose between open or traditional schools. They can select what is best for their children from each. Only by understanding the differences intellectually, rather than emotionally, can they begin to do that.

Dear Mrs. Miller:
    I am interested to see that this year's Teacher of the Year, like last year's, is a far cry from Back to Basics. She

leans to "way out" methods rather than traditional and seems more interested in the child's self-image than in achievement. How come?

Mrs. R. J. L.

Dear Mrs. L.:

Elaine Barbour and Myrra Lee represent the best in American teaching—that is why they were elected Teacher of the Year. Fortunately, such teachers can be found in every state. They are secure enough to avoid jumping on educational bandwagons like Back to Basics. They are committed to the belief that learning grows in a child who is having fun, who dares to question, and who has enough sense of worth to make mistakes. They are also creative enough to innovate. Teachers who rigidly adhere to traditional teaching, or who consider the three R's the most important part of learning, probably lack Teacher of the Year qualities. Parent support may en-able more teachers to be Elaine Barbours and Myrra Lees.

Dear Mrs. Miller:

My husband and I feel that the teachers in our children's school are so busy listening to the children that they don't ever *tell* them anything. Whatever happened to the idea that teachers impart learning? Is there anything we can do?

Basic Parents

Dear Basic Parents:

Teachers still impart learning . . . but not only to the mind. A teacher from Texas writes her teaching goal on the blackboard so she and her students never lose sight of what is important in the classroom. She writes: "I-A-L-A-C." These letters stand for: "I Am Loved And Capa-ble." She believes, as most good teachers do, that stu-dents need to learn that as much as their ABC's.

Is there anything you can do? Yes. Realize that truly basic education begins with a good self-image, not with

the alphabet, and extends far beyond the classroom into
living. That makes you imparters of learning, too.

Dear Mrs. Miller:

I am interested in finding out why the dress code of the
60s is completely gone. I believe that if our children are
dressed for play, that is what they do, and if they are well
dressed, they will behave better.

Mrs. F.

Dear Mrs. F.:

The dress code was abandoned when educational in-
novations were undertaken to give students more deci-
sion-making powers and to make school more a part of
their real life. At the same time, Civil Rights was ex-
tended to include students as a minority group; one of
their rights was to dress and wear their hair as they
wished. With the recent Back to Basics swing, many
schools are reinstating dress codes . . . and many of them
are being sued on the issue of civil rights.

Dear Mrs. Miller:

Do you think it is fair to put those strict new requirements into schools? Doesn't it mean that a lot of kids will fail
those tests and never get a high school diploma?

R. D.

Dear R. D.:

I don't call the new requirements strict—I call them
realistic. And I think they are fairer than giving a kid a
high school diploma that has no meaning. We do not
help a young person by pretending he has learned; we
only help him by letting him really learn. If our high
school diploma becomes more than a Wizard of Oz piece
of paper, perhaps educators will begin to do the job of
educating. I think it is high time schools set up stan-

dards for graduation . . . that they use every modern
method of reinforcement and individualized teaching to
enable kids to meet those standards . . . but that they do
not pretend when kids do not meet them. If students
cannot meet graduation standards, let educators devise
new teaching methods so that they can.

Dear Mrs. Miller:
You seem so against everything in education—marks,
Back to Basics, teacher authority, etc. I'd like to know one
thing: what are you *for?*

Anonymous

Dear Anonymous:
I am for basic skills as a tool, not as an end in them-
selves. I am for learning through discovery, not through
playing back what someone else said. I am for integrated
schools which reflect the real world. I am for reading the
classics because their language is beautiful and their
characters are real. I am for grammar because it helps
children express themselves. I am for student voice in
school decision-making because students are the major
part of a school community. I am for independent study
because real learning always takes place alone. I am for
individualized teaching so that children can go where
and how and when learning works for them. I am for
eliminating marks because they stigmatize failure, which
is an essential to learning. I am for signing one's name to
letters . . . because it shows the courage of one's convic-
tions.

8/Evaluating Your School

In 1972, Christopher Jencks and his team stunned the educational world with a new study entitled *Inequality: A Reassessment of the Effect of Family and Schooling in America.* "Variations in what children learn in school," he wrote in a summary of his findings, "depend largely on variations in what they bring to school, not on variation in what schools offer them. . . . The result achieved by a school depends largely on a single input—the characteristic of the entering child." In short, there is no such thing as a good school or a bad school—only good or bad learners.

In addition to the controversy he aroused, mainly from minority groups whose children Jencks had apparently condemned as nonlearners, many parents felt that he had left them stranded with sole responsibility for learning. Good teachers, bad teachers, basic or open schools, facilities or no facilities—nothing mattered. Only genes and those first few years at home.

Refusing to accept this preordained approach, some parents continued their struggles with schools and school systems, and in 1979 help came in the form of a British study under the direction of Dr. Michael Rutter, whose findings were in direct opposition to those of Jencks. Examining similar schools with similar student bodies in one of Britain's low socioeconomic districts, the British team found that "school differences were not just a reflection of intake patterns and that much of the effects of schools were linked with their features as social organizations." What matters most, they found, is the overall tone of the school and teacher-student relationships in which the expectation is for follow-through and success.

They came to the conclusion that the school *did* make a difference.

What most parents have believed all along was thus confirmed: that both they and the school *share* responsibility for their children's learning. That is why they have fought with schools—to make them do a job worthy of their children. And that is why they have fought with their children too—to make them do a job worthy of themselves.

Without knowing it, parents evaluate schools in a variety of ways. Whenever they move from one city to another, they case the school situation before deciding on a neighborhood; many an extra bedroom and finished basement have been traded in favor of a good teacher. In some cases, parents are willing to pay for the privilege of sending their children out of the district if they see greener fields and better schools there.

The voucher system, which has recently gained favor in some states, was developed as a result of parents' increasingly critical attitudes toward schools. Under the system, vouchers are issued to parents in the amount of the state's cost of educating a child. Parents are then able to apply the vouchers to any school they wish—be it public, independent, or religious. The hope is that this system will force poorer schools to upgrade themselves under the selective scrutiny of parents, but whether it will afford opportunities for minority children to attend better schools or relegate them forever to the worst remains a moot question.

The ultimate in parental evaluation has been evidenced in the number of court suits that have sprung up in recent years. One family sued because, on graduation from high school, their son could only read at fourth-grade level. Another sued because their high school graduate was unable to fill out an application form. Whether they won or lost their case, what these parents were saying in court was simply, "This school failed."

IDENTIFYING STRENGTHS AND WEAKNESSES

The strongest reason parents have for evaluating a school is to identify its strengths and weaknesses in the hope of effecting change. They are, however, not alone in their efforts to do this. Every accredited school in the country belongs to a regional accrediting association that evaluates it every ten years. High schools have had to be accredited for years; junior high and elementary schools have had more leeway. Parents should check to see whether their school is accredited and, if not, apply pressure toward that end.

The association's evaluation process usually starts a year in advance, involving teachers, staff, and administrators in committee work and self-analysis. The school is visited by a group of educators from other schools, who spend long days and nights investigating all aspects of the school and compiling a report. The preliminary report is then read to the assembled school community, pointing out major strengths and weaknesses. A full report focusing on each department specifically is sent some time later.

By the end of the evaluation, the school community—even students, who have been on their best behavior—is exhausted, but often wiser. In five years' time the school must report on changes effected in response to the evaluators' recommendations. In ten years, they undergo the entire process again.

There are two viewpoints from which evaluations can be made. The accrediting association measures a school against its own goals and philosophy—not against the association's idea of what a school should be, but against the school's own definition. Thus, if the school states as its objective the development of the total child, the evaluators will judge the effectiveness of its program in supporting that objective. Similarly, if the school aim is to stress academics, the evaluators will judge it in relation to that aim. They evaluate the effectiveness of the school, not its purpose.

A second, more subjective, kind of evaluation is more applicable to parents. It measures the strengths and weaknesses of a school according to the goal and philosophy of those evaluating it—in most cases, parents. Thus, the parent who wants a varied and effective program will come up with a different evaluation from the parent who looks solely for academics.

Schools—like cities—are complex organizations. One can

stroll through New York, Chicago, or Los Angeles, collecting impressions, and leave feeling that the city is cold or friendly, safe or dangerous, clean or dirty, depending on the quality of one's experiences. Subjective and superficial as they are, however, such findings have little validity. Similarly, as parents subjectively evaluating a school on the basis of hearsay and scattered observations you may feel that you are making an honest judgment, but more likely your findings will reinforce the feelings you began with, since it is human tendency to see what one expects to see.

An honest evaluation of a school must be conducted with greater thought and effort. A good starting point is to understand the avoidance of pitfalls that parents inevitably meet. The following lists are intended to help direct you around them.

Here are some of the things you should avoid doing:

1. Don't consider your children's complaints about school as a valid evaluation.
2. Don't accept rumors as evidence of a school problem.
3. Don't undertake the evaluation with hostility.
4. Don't look only for negative aspects of the school.
5. Don't be secretive about what you are doing.

And keep the following positive points in mind:

1. Think of yourself as part of the school team, not as an alien.
2. Undertake the evaluation positively as a way to help the school.
3. Explain to administrators, teachers, and staff what you are doing before you begin.
4. Plan the steps in your evaluation before beginning it.
5. Record the strengths of the school as well as the weaknesses.
6. Write down your findings as you go along; do not rely on memory.

Planning the Evaluation

Pitfalls thus avoided, parents can take the first step: planning the evaluation. What do you want to evaluate? The school, of course, but that is a complex institution. What aspects of the school? There are many. The following categories are the major ones parents want to investigate in studying a school. The questions listed under each heading are intended merely to serve as suggestions, the kinds of things you will want to look for. Your own concerns and the unique situation in each school will enable you to formulate many more questions of your own.

Goals

1. What does the school hope to accomplish for each student?
2. Are teachers aware of this goal?
3. Are they in agreement with it?
4. What has been done to make parents aware of school goals?
5. Are parents in agreement with them?
6. Who has been involved in setting the goals?
7. What is the school doing in every area to achieve these goals?

Teachers

1. What is their training, background, and previous experience?
2. How do their salary and benefits compare with those of teachers in other districts?
3. Have they gone on strike? If so, how recently? Why? With what results?
4. What is the teacher turnover in the school? Why?
5. What is the teacher load? How much free time?
6. How are teachers evaluated by the principal?
7. What are their attitudes toward achievement? Failure? Parents? Other teachers? The school administration? The community?
8. How flexible are they in changing plans and relinquishing schedules?
9. How do they relate to the students?
10. What is the atmosphere in their classrooms?

Students

1. Is there a heterogeneous student body?
2. Do *all* students interrelate, sharing their differences?
3. What is the attendance rate?
4. How do students feel about the school?
5. How do students relate to teachers?
6. Do they participate in school activities?
7. How does their achievement compare to that of other schools?
8. How do they behave in school?
9. Are students "tracked" in classes?

Administration

1. What is the principal's attitude toward people?
2. On what basis are teachers hired?
3. Is the school run autocratically or democratically?
4. How are disciplinary problems handled?
5. Is the principal committed to an educational philosophy? What is it?
6. Is the principal supportive of teachers? Students? Parents?
7. How long has the principal been there?
8. How welcome are parents, students, and teachers in the school office?

Parents

1. Is there an active Parents' Association?
2. Do parents serve as volunteer aides in the school?
3. Are parents welcome to visit classrooms?
4. How do parents feel about the school?
5. How does the school feel about parents?
6. Is there good communication between home and school?

School Board

1. Who are the board members? Do they reflect the community?

2. Does the board have sufficient money to provide what the school needs?
3. What are the board's educational concerns?
4. How does the board feel about your school compared to others?
5. Does the board work closely with the community?

Curriculum

1. Are there required courses in high school? Which ones?
2. Is there a variety of electives?
3. Do teachers stress basic skills—especially reading?
4. Does the curriculum encourage creativity?
5. Does it provide remedial help for students having trouble?
6. Are there Advanced Placement courses? Programs for the gifted?
7. What are the offerings in arts, sciences, languages?
8. Does the physical education program provide adequately for non-athletes?
9. Is independent study available for all students?
10. Are courses taught through inquiry? Textbooks? Lectures? Class discussions?
11. Are source papers required?
12. Do all courses, not just English courses, demand standards of writing?
13. Are students used to help teach each other?
14. Is credit given for work-study programs outside school?

Extracurricular Activities

1. Are there opportunities for every student to be involved in activities?
2. Can students do volunteer work in the community?
3. Is the community brought into the school to participate in extracurricular activities?
4. Has the school newspaper freedom to express student opinions?
5. Does the school support extracurricular programs with money? Teachers? Administrative enthusiasm?

6. Does the student body support them?
7. Do the parents support them?

Measurement of Student Progress

1. How often are reports sent to parents?
2. Are interim notices sent to parents when children have problems?
3. Are parents notified when children make special contributions?
4. What kind of evaluative criteria are used: tests, classwork, homework, class participation, final exams, term papers? How much emphasis is put on each?
5. Are students involved in evaluating themselves?
6. Are marks used? What kinds? Is effort evaluated?
7. Are students competitive? Are teachers? Are parents?
8. Are comment slips sent home? Are they detailed? Helpful?
9. What motivates students to work?

Guidance

1. Are guidance counselors available?
2. How many students per guidance counselor?
3. Do they do career and college counseling?
4. Do they value the non-college-bound student equally with the college-bound one?
5. Do they do personal counseling?
6. Do they do group counseling in human relations?
7. Does the school have sex education? At what levels? Who teaches it? What material is covered? How is it taught?
8. Is there a psychologist or a psychiatrist on staff?

Physical Plant

1. Is it clean? Do you see graffiti?
2. Is it in good repair?
3. Is it light? Well-ventilated? Safe?
4. Is there adequate space?
5. Is there a library? How many books has it? Do students use it? When?

6. Is there a media center? What equipment is available? When do students use it?
7. What audiovisual aids are available to teachers? Do they know how to use them? How often do they use them? In what ways?

Community

1. Do the student body and the faculty reflect the makeup of the community?
2. What percentage of teachers live in the community?
3. Do students do volunteer work in the community?
4. Does the school share its facilities with the community?
5. How does the community feel about the school?
6. How does the community act toward the school?
7. How does the school act toward the community?

Graduates

1. What percentage of students goes to college? What kinds of colleges? What is their success rate there?
2. What percentage of students goes to specialized schools? What kinds of schools?
3. What percentage of students goes straight into jobs? Why? What kinds of jobs? What happens to them in their jobs?
4. What percentage gets married right away? Girls? Boys? What do they do after marriage?
5. What level of reading is required for graduation?
6. What is the drop-out rate before graduation?

Following these guidelines, a parent or a PTA will be able to pursue an evaluation that will produce a clear and reliable picture of a school.

Obviously, not every parent can undertake such a thorough evaluation alone. The family wanting to check schools before settling in a specific area has only limited time and facilities with which to investigate. Parents can, however, visit the school on several occasions, making appointments to talk with a sampling of teachers, administrators, students, parents, and a board member. The areas of their concern will be the same as those just enumerated, but their examination will necessarily be on a smaller scale.

CARRYING OUT THE EVALUATION

After planning comes the actual doing. How do parents get all the answers to their questions needed for an in-depth school evaluation? The following steps will help:

Work through the PTA if possible. If the PTA does not support your evaluation, work with a smaller group within the PTA that does support it. Setting up a school-wide evaluation alone is hazardous.

Involve the entire school community in your evaluation. Do not limit it to parents—first, because they will not get an inside view of the school without inside help; and second, because they will alienate everybody who is not included. Therefore, encourage teachers, administrators, students, and the Board of Education to join the team. Many of them may be as concerned about the school as you are. Even those who are not and merely want to retain the status quo will usually not defy the suggestion of self-evaluation. They may try to turn it into self-defense instead, but you will get further working ostensibly *with* them rather than blatantly *against* them.

Appoint committees. Committees that cut across lines are the most effective—that is, ones composed of representatives from all areas of the school community. They should, however, be kept small; large committees get little done. Appoint a strong chairperson to head each committee, one who will work hard and will get committee members to do the same. Assign a specific area to each committee for investigation, being careful not to overlap.

Ask questions. Do not be afraid to ask questions of people in the school—remember, you are on their side. If they are reluctant to answer, explain your purpose. If you run into outright hostility, don't persist; you can probably secure the information you need from another source. If, however, the administration tries to block the investigation entirely, try to enlist support from higher up. Educational systems have a well-defined hierarchy: from teacher to principal to superintendent to board of education to state commissioner to United States commissioner. Only the President and the Secretary of Education stand higher than that.

Listen. When people talk to you, listen to what they say. Don't be so eager to ask your next question that you lose track of what they are telling you. Also, listen to people whom you do *not* question: students talking together, teachers in a classroom, parents waiting to pick up children, the principal with members of the staff. The way they relate in the normal course of affairs gives you a clue to school attitudes and morale.

Observe. Seeing is evaluating too. Watch your own children as they go to school in the morning and tackle their homework at night. Look at the faces of teachers and students as they walk down the hall or sit in class or leave the building at the end of the day. Study bulletin boards to see what kinds of notices are posted. Look at parents during open school days and at students in assembly.

Take notes. Do not trust your memory to pull out what you have learned when you need to write a report. You may have forgotten. Keep notes as you go along and insist that the rest of the evaluating team do the same. Keep a record of dates of interviews and observations too. You may need them for future reference or verification.

Write a report. Findings not solidified in a report tend to get lost. After committees have completed their investigations, an appointed member from each committee should work together on a report. The report should be organized by area of investigation, with the findings clearly highlighted. A concise report will be read, understood, and remembered.

DEFINING A GOOD SCHOOL

When all the measurements are taken and all the reports written, when committees dissolve and parents return to worrying about report cards, one question remains: What is a good school? Volumes have been written in answer.

A good school is one that gives your child what you consider important. There are those who advocate highly structured schools and those who want the radical innovation of a Summerhill. There are those who say, "Let school teach academics; I'll teach the rest at home," and those who turn their children over to schools in loco parentis. No simple definition of a good school or a bad school exists: we know which is which by being involved with schools; seeing what they do to our children.

When we see our children crushed, turned off, standardized, when they cannot read or write and enjoy nothing but television, when they grow tense over failure and hate themselves, all indicators point to a bad school. When our children are happy, curious, and excited about learning, when they read alone for fun and write poetry and try to discover things, when they are unafraid to make mistakes and eager to try something new, when they like their teachers, we know we have a good school.

America is not without good schools—in towns, cities, and rural areas spotted from coast to coast. Often they are unknown beyond their community, unacclaimed as they—in all their variety—give children the best in education. I have seen such schools on an Indian reservation, on a university campus, in the heart of a big city, in our southeastern tip in Florida, in the snowbound state of Washington, in the elegant suburbs and in the not too distant ghetto.

Drawing on my experience in observing these and other schools, I have tried to establish their common denominators, put them together, and come up with what seems to me the ideal school. This school does not exist as such. It is a composite of excellent schools that some of America's children are fortunate enough to attend.

Goals

The entire school community has discussed and put in writing what the aims of the school are: "We believe in the uniqueness of all children, in the excitement with which they discover, in the strength they gain from trying, failing, and trying again, and in their ability to help themselves and others grow through sharing. The goal of our school is to enable children to develop in all dimensions of their being according to these beliefs so that they may live in wonder and wisdom, learning and love."

Teachers

The teachers are highly trained professionals, receiving good salaries and benefits, and having good working conditions. They do not limit their teaching, preparation, or extra hours to union demands but give unstintingly from the commitment they have made to education. They use existing materials creatively and, in addition, create their own. They hold high standards for students to meet, following through on them meticulously. They individualize a large part of their teaching and are ready to forgo lesson plans when student interest leads them into unexpected areas of learning. They care about students as individuals, relating to them as equal human beings, though not as "pals." They are happy to be teaching at this school.

Students

The students represent a cross section of the community where the school is located, working together in all classes, activities, and social affairs. Through student council and appointed committees, they participate actively in decision-making on matters of curriculum, teachers, schedules, extra-curricular activities, and community involvement. They are excited by the idea of learning and pursue individualized work and independent study in subjects of their own interest. Although they look forward to good report cards, they do not feel under pressure to achieve, being motivated by self-satisfaction rather than by competition. And though they like classes, they prefer their involvement in music, art, drama, film, computers, and sports. They also enjoy volunteer work in the community, for which they receive credit. They do not label each other "bright" or "dumb," since everyone works at an individual pace, and no one is regarded as a failure. The students consider themselves lucky to be at this school.

Administration

The principal is a strong team leader, involving the entire school community in decisions and then, as school head, assuming responsibility for them, standing behind both ideas and teachers against any opposition that may arise. Everyone feels free to walk into the school office and discuss concerns or offer suggestions. The principal believes in excellence and is committed, with the school, to its pursuit. The principal believes in human dignity, valuing people above marks or money. He or she has been at the school about eight years and does not plan to leave.

Parents

An active Parents' Association keeps parents involved and informed on all matters of school operation. Parents consider themselves part of the team and, as such, work for the school—raising money, planning programs, serving as volunteers. Lines of communication between parents and school are always open; there is no need for telephone gossip. Seeing their children happy and learning, these parents love the school, never wanting to move away.

School Board

School board seats are heartily contended for at every election. The members, representing a cross section of the district, care about educating children and devote much time to this goal to assure the success of the schools in their jurisdiction. They fight for adequate funds, being unwilling to cut enrichment courses that other schools consider "frills." They make frequent visits to the schools in their district, taking particular pride in this one.

Curriculum

The curriculum is varied enough to meet the needs and special interests of all students—including the gifted, the special, the college-bound, the career-oriented, the culturally diverse, and those geared toward specialized disciplines. In the lower grades it shares the emphasis between basic skills and the arts and human relationships. Reinforcement is available to any child in difficulty. At the upper levels the curriculum emphasizes approaches to study more heavily than course content per se. Its aim in all subjects is to develop lifelong learners. The curriculum demands standards of excellence, leaving no room for "getting by just this once" on the part of either students or faculty. There is no tracking: individualized teaching precludes it.

Extracurricular Activities

Extracurricular activities are developed according to the interests of students and teachers, who take the initiative for organizing programs. In this way, any kind of activity is possible as long as there are people willing to become involved. Although supervised by teachers, activities are student-run—even the school newspaper, which is allowed to voice opinions differing from those of the administration—as long as it does so in proper English!

Guidance

The school has one full-time guidance counselor for every hundred students. Counselors are available to students at any time for personal counseling or for discussion of school matters. The guidance department offers programs for students as well—career guidance, human relations, love and marriage—in addition to discussion groups in which students share their concerns. In high school, the guidance counselors meet with parents and students regularly to help plan what comes after graduation. There is a staff psychiatrist who visits the school weekly for a regular meeting with the guidance counselors and also meets with individual students and teachers when requested. Often parents are invited to sit in.

Physical Plant

The building of this school is nothing to rave about, but it is bright, airy, and clean. Though it may not be quite roomy enough, students and teachers find usable space in the yard, basement, and hallways. Improvising brings them closer together somehow. Fortunately, the library is large, filled with invitingly displayed books—many of them paperbacks—and individual carrels for study. Along one side are private booths with audiovisual aids and teaching programs in constant use by the students. The principal and the Board of Education say, "One of these days we'll be able to build a new school," but it does not really matter. This one works fine.

Community

Reflecting the community, this school is very much a part of it. Students work at the local hospital, block associations, at a school for the deaf and a home for the aged. Since many teachers live in the community within a few blocks of the school, students meet them in a non-school framework—shopping, churchgoing, and so on. The school offers the community courses in literature and computer and shares with it a theater group, a chorus, and a debating team. At the annual block party the school turns its cafeteria into a restaurant, and throughout the year the local sports groups use the gymnasium at night. The school has never been vandalized.

Graduates

Seventy percent of the students go to college after graduation—some to community colleges, others to a range of four-year colleges. A small percentage gets married right away; 10 percent enters specialized schools of art, fashion, or technology. The remaining ones take jobs, mainly because of financial need, and many of these attend college at night and eventually earn a degree. In order to graduate, a student must read at the eleventh-grade level; most can. Those students unable to meet the requirement receive a certificate rather than a diploma.

I have not sketched this imaginary school simply as an exercise in fantasy. I have drawn it, rather, to give a clear picture for parents to keep in mind when measuring their own school's qualities. Let it serve as an ideal model—not one to imitate, for that would be impossible, but from which to draw and learn.

When you evaluate your school, use a long-term measurement. Be guarded in changes you want to make. Certainly, whether Shakespeare is taught in eighth or tenth grade or homework begins in first or second matters little in the test of time. What a child *is* matters forever. Concentrate on emphasizing that goal; encourage the school to help students grow into fulfilled human beings.

As one teacher said, "We don't teach subjects; we teach children. So human beings, not subjects, emerge." Let that philosophy be the lesson plan for your school.

Dear Mrs. Miller:

We are contemplating moving either to Colorado Springs, Colorado, or Richardson, Texas. We have three school age children—elementary, junior high, and high school. Is there any way of finding out the better schools in these areas?

Mr. J. B.

Dear Mr. B.:

It is difficult to know a school from the outside. However, there are steps you can take that will help you. First, decide what you think constitutes a good school. Is it the curriculum? The teaching methods? Philosophy? Goals? Is it college acceptances? The kinds of people that teach? Next, write to the Commissioner of Educaton of each state you are considering. Explain what you are looking for in a school and ask him which district comes closest to matching your requirements. If possible, you and your child should visit the school before deciding. Talk to the principal, to teachers and students, to some parents who have to come to pick up their children. What feeling do you get from the school? Is the atmosphere happy? Busy? Are there signs of vandalism? How's the library? How are the classrooms arranged? None of this is foolproof, but it should help you to decide.

Dear Mrs. Miller:

Please send me any information you have on how to determine quality in education in schools. Thank you for your help.

M. A. H.

Dear M. A. H.:

That's like asking, "Tell me about the world." But I'll try.

1. Look inside the school. *Is the atmosphere alive? Are the walls covered with student activities and artwork? Do the students look involved? Are the teachers in the rooms when they have no classes? Is the library a busy place? Does it have a lot of paperbacks? Audiovisual? Are students and teachers talking together?*

2. Talk to the principal, teachers, and students. *Do they seem genuinely enthusiastic? Can they define their goals? Do many of the students go on to good colleges? Are there programs for the gifted? Do they offer independent study? Advanced Placement? Several languages? Art? Music? Theater? Community work?*

3. Sit in on classes if you can. *Is there discussion rather than lecture? Is it animated? Are the teacher and students prepared? Are they having fun?*

A Yes *to all the above is a good sign. How many* No's *you can afford depends on you . . . and on your alternatives. Good Luck!*

Dear Mrs. Miller:

I think my children are being cheated on their education because the schools in our town are pretty bad. I know that towns around are much better. They are in the same state, so how come? More important, what can I do?

J. V.

Dear J. V.:

Your question is valid and can be raised in every state in the country. In fact, it is *being raised. Communities that collect school taxes based on real estate values—wealthy suburbs, for instance—spend more money for education and have, therefore, good schools. Communities with lower school revenue based on lower real estate values fare less well. State governments where this system is in effect are becoming aware of the discrepancies and are proposing a reallocation of state tax money. By giving more to the low school tax districts and less to*

the high ones, they will, they feel, equalize schools in the
state. As for what you can do, first check to learn how
your town raises school funds. Then write, phone, or
make an appointment with a state legislator to share
your opinions.

Dear Mrs. Miller:
    We live in a big city and have to send our children
(Grades three, six, and eight) to schools that are terrible. The
classes are too big; the teaching is poor, and the learning is
way below grade level. For our eldest child, the school isn't
even safe. What about private school? How do you find a good
one? And what's the story on scholarships?

                                            Mr. and Mrs. S. L.

Dear Mr. and Mrs. L.:
    I weep for the millions of children in this country
caught in the same situation as yours. Unfortunately,
there aren't enough private schools and not nearly
enough scholarship money to ease the problem for more
than a small percentage. However, try. Start, if you wish,
with a school of your religious affiliation. Then write for
information to the National Association of Independent
Schools, 18 Tremont Street, Boston, Massachusetts
02108. A visit to each school they send you will let you
know the scholarship situation. If it doesn't work out,
supplement your children's education at home—with
books and discussions, trips, and visits to museums. In
addition, kick up a storm with your city and state Board
of Education, mayor and governor and Commissioner of
Education. As a last resort, move to a better school dis-
trict.

9/Making Changes in Your School

Ellie and Joel Patman are moving. They hate to leave the 150-acre farm in eastern Pennsylvania into which they sank their savings five years ago. Nan, their four-year-old, will miss Kelly the cow, whom she greets every morning with a hug; Eric, too, will miss his rides on their old dapple. Ellie and Joel forsook the city where they grew up for a lifetime on the farm and will miss the million reasons why: the garden they struggle over, wild raspberries on the hill, evening walks when the air is cool, and the misty morning sunrises. They will miss naked swims in the pond, lessons learned from trees and from the wind and stars, and wide-open meadows where snakes hide.

They are moving to the suburbs on a street lined with ranch houses. It has a good school.

"If the children attend their local school," Joel says, "it will destroy everything they have learned growing up. Those rigid little desks in rows and pictures colored within the lines will stifle them. Nature allows room, you know."

Ellie agrees. "The new school is good—open and individualized. The kids love it already just from our visit." She adds wistfully, "We can always take trips to the country."

"Why change where you live?" I ask Ellie. "Why not stay and change the school instead?"

She and Joel look appalled at the suggestion, gasping in unison, "Change the school! What's the point in trying?"

But there *is* a point.

Parents are effecting changes in their schools in increasing numbers throughout the country. No longer are they willing to remain passive bystanders, watching their children herded into classrooms they consider destructive under the guidance of teachers they consider incapable. They themselves are taking the lead so that their children will be educated as they determine.

"They're *my* children," a mother explains. "Why should people who don't know them and don't care about them decide how they will be educated? They don't decide how they will be fed or housed or treated medically. They're damn well not going to decide about their education."

The American Federation of Teachers meets this growing militarism of parents with disdain, referring to parents as "self-appointed judges." But recently, the National School Boards Association publicly stated, "We believe in lay control of education, not control by professionals." Under that banner, families who feel like the Patmans can draw strength to march instead of move.

Their greatest ally is the PTA. What used to be ample-bosomed subject matter for cartoonists has today become a decision-making force in major educational issues. No longer are cookie sales and clothing exchanges focal points of PTA efforts; parents are now getting involved in the philosophical and operational core of the school itself.

The metamorphosis started in 1972 when, at an annual convention, the National PTA reexamined its bylaws, particularly one that stated, "Local chapters should cooperate with schools . . . in ways that will not interfere with the administration." Parents were being told to cause no waves! But times had changed since the PTA's birth in 1897; issues had arisen on which parents had strong feelings. For instance, many of them wanted integrated schools and curriculums and textbooks that treated minority groups with equality and dignity. They wanted courses to make children aware of their environment and aware of themselves as individuals relating to one another.

Such issues caused waves because administrators did not always agree. If PTA members followed the bylaws, they would have to back off from issues that mattered to them; if, on the other hand, they fought school administrators, they would be disobeying their bylaws. A dilemma?

No, a solvable problem. The National PTA changed the bylaws. Throwing out the old noninterference clause, it replaced it with hands-on action. PTA policy became, and continues strongly, "to seek to participate in the decision-making process establishing school policy." Wave-making became permissible. Since then, local PTAs have gone so far as to organize parent strikes, boycotts, and lawsuits in their determination to make decisions in *their* schools concerning *their* children's education.

Steps in the Process

The majority of PTAs find success through less hostile means, however. The process they use is one with which parents should familiarize themselves and follow to effect changes in a child's school. From start to finish it looks something like this:

1. A parent is dissatisfied. Dissatisfaction can stem from any number of sources: Parents may see their child unhappy in school, or may disagree with the administration's philosophy of education, or may see gaps in the curriculum, or may consider a teacher destructive. Whatever the specific area of concern, you believe that your child is not getting the proper education.

2. The parent talks to the PTA president. Take your concern to a person in charge—usually the president, but in some cases the chairperson of the Complaint Committee. It will be discussed informally. Perhaps other parents have reported similar concerns, which are already under investigation. Perhaps you have pointed out a weakness in the school no one has previously been aware of. (On the other hand, if you are thought to be a chronic complainer, blaming the school whenever problems arise with your child, you will be calmed with reassurances.) If so, the issue will be put on the agenda for the next PTA meeting.

3. The PTA discusses the concern. The PTA president presents, or asks you to present, the school issue that concerns you. Either way, it is done objectively, with no name-calling and with as little anger as possible. Discussion is opened to the floor, and parents (and teachers) share their responses to the issue presented. Discussion ends with three possible courses: The matter may be dropped for lack of support; there may be agreement on the need for action; or they may appoint a committee for further investigation.

4. If the PTA drops the matter. If the general body of the PTA decides to pursue the matter no further— for lack of interest or support or for fear of stirring up trouble—you may decide to drop the matter too. In the course of discussion, you may even have been convinced that your worries were groundless. If, however, you are still determined to follow through, you can do so in two ways:

You can tackle the problem alone. This does not mean waging a telephone campaign of rumor, gossip, and malice in order to enlist support. It means conscientious planning and hard work to investigate on your own in order to bring the matter up again at another PTA meeting. This time you will have more specific details and may be able to convince the group to support your concerns and undertake an investigation.

Alternatively, you can tackle the problem with a small group within the PTA. Even when the general body does not support a parent concern, a minority group may—and usually does. This group can become a nucleus within the school, contacting members of the school community for support in its efforts for change. Your group must never work in secret, but should openly notify the PTA, the administration, the faculty, and the Board of Education. The committees should, whenever possible, include members of all areas of the school community. What begins as a small group effort may end as a full-scale school undertaking after all.

5. If the PTA endorses action . . . When the PTA votes to support your original concern, it sets in motion wheels that roll toward change. The usual procedure that would be followed (as outlined in the preceding chapter) is to form committees to handle an investigation of various areas of the school's operation, to conduct a school-wide evaluation, and to present a report to the school body.

After results of the school evaluation have been presented and discussed with the school community, committees meet again to draw up suggestions. It is wise to invite nonmembers to contribute ideas, thus assuring a wider range of suggestions and greater support later on when their suggestions are offered for approval. All suggestions should be checked for feasibility before being presented.

Suggestions are more likely to be accepted by the school when they are presented positively. Criticism only builds defenses that can stand firm against any kind of change. The differences can be seen in the cases of two hypothetical PTAs which decided that their schools needed to add computer courses to the curriculum.

The president of one PTA announced after its evaluation, "We are way behind the times. Other schools have computers. What's wrong with our school?" The principal, instead of addressing the issue of the computer, spent the rest of the meeting proving that there was nothing wrong with the school. When, at the end, a parent moved that the school add a computer course, the Board of Education voted the motion down on the basis of inadequate funds. Everybody left the meeting feeling angry.

The president of a second PTA was more tactful. "Our school stands for the best in modern education," she began. "Wouldn't the inclusion of computer courses reinforce our aim?"

The principal agreed, accepting the kudos graciously. The Board of Education agreed too but balked at the cost.

"Let me look into possibilities," the principal offered. "Maybe I can find a less expensive way."

As a result, the school tied a telephone line into a central computer, used in two new course offerings, while the Board of Education began requisitioning state funds to purchase the school's own computer.

Implementing Changes

When a school implements PTA suggestions, everyone is usually happy. The danger that may arise, however, is that parents may become arrogant in their newfound power. If this happens, the cause is lost, for members of a school community cannot work together in the competitive atmosphere that will brew. A school is a team, and only as a team can it operate successfully. When any one group—be it parents or administrators—assumes the position of *winner* over *loser*, it sets up hostile camps. Change cannot be effective, or even effected, in a school where any group feels, "My side won." *Our* side must win, and our side is the entire school.

On the other hand, when a school refuses to implement PTA suggestions, different dangers arise. One is that parents will grow angry and in their anger work against the school. But the ultimate losers in the battle between parents and school are the children. Instead of fighting, parents will help their children more by coolly persisting in their efforts.

Another danger is that parents will grow apathetic in the future to effect changes they have planned and worked for. They may give up, sighing, "What's the point of trying?" But there is always a point. If the first PTA attempt fails, a second may work—or a third. Determined parents can change a principal's mind, can convert a Board of Education, can reeducate a teacher—*if* they persist with facts and a businesslike approach. When they cannot, they can seek the support from higher sources, as suggested in the previous chapter as a way to overcome a school's refusal to cooperate with an evaluation.

Although it is not easy for parents to enlist support from authorities above their own school, it can be done—and has been done. In some cases, these authorities merely want to keep peace and find that soothing the voices of parents will make life easier for them. In other cases, they themselves are aware of problems in the school and need only this final push to get them to take action.

Unfortunately, in still other cases the authorities turn a deaf ear. Perhaps they don't care. In that case, parents armed with facts and figures face a challenge to *make* them care. Perhaps, however, they support the school's position against that of the parents. If so, only an all-out effort by numbers of parents great enough to shake the authority's security can have any real effect. A show of strength through letters, telegrams, and group meetings is far more likely to succeed than a strike. It is worthwhile for parents to try to reach higher authorities when they are blocked at lower levels. Here is what the educational hierarchy looks like in most states:

The Superintendent of Schools. The superintendent is responsible for the operation of all schools within the district, with authority to hire, fire, and transfer principals. The superintendent therefore has power to effect immediate change within a school.

The Board of Education. Although parents may have been working closely with their Board of Education, or with a single board member, they should still consider it as a higher-level ally. The Board of Education is powerful because it controls the money allocated to schools and determines broad educational policy.

The State Chief School Officer. The person who heads up the state Department of Education is usually the Commissioner of Education; in some states, he is called the State School Superintendent. He determines educational policy on the highest level throughout the state, mandating certain courses, setting requirements for high school graduation, teacher certification, and funds allocated locally. The Chief Officer, or, more likely, member of the staff, will see PTA representatives on appointment.

The State Senate Chairperson of the Education Committee. The Senate Education Committee presents all bills for funds for education in the state. It is, therefore, in a position to bring new courses into the curriculum, eliminate existing ones, change student-teacher ratio, overhaul the entire educational approach.

The State Assembly (or House of Representatives) Chairperson of the Educational Committee. Like the Senate Education Committee, this one proposes bills to appropriate, or cut down on, funds for education. How the body's vote goes depends on the chairperson's ability to persuade fellow Assembly members to support the committee's recommendations. How your vote goes determines whether the chairperson returns to the Assembly.

AREAS OF CHANGE

Working for change through these steps, parents (individually or through PTAs and Parent Associations) have been able to become decisive voices in the education of their children. The old focus of change, based on what was called "morality," was often *anti*-education, leading to book burnings and censorship. The new way, based on intelligent examination, is *pro*-education.

Parents are demanding schools in which their children can learn. The changes they are bringing to their schools focus on five main areas. The following examples have been chosen to give some idea of what is happening across the country.

Finances

Since money in large measure determines what a school can and cannot do, parental focus on financial changes is effective:

• In New Jersey, high school parents considered the long delays in receiving their children's progress reports a sign of ineffective administration. On investigating, they discovered that a shortage of clerical help frustrated the principal as much as it did them. They persuaded the Board of Education to allocate additional funds for office help.

• Parents in a large Eastern city pressured the mayor and the chief of police to hire additional school guards when they felt their children's safety was at stake.

• In California, the PTA of a school got hold of a copy of the teachers' proposed contract with a demand for a 16 percent increase in salary. Realizing that funds allocated to so large a teacher increment would necessitate curtailments in curriculums and special faculty, they opposed the contract. They won.

• One of the most controversial financial issues parents are involved in today concerns the funds from which schools are financed. As public-spirited citizens, parents have brought to light the inequity of current funding through local property taxes. This, they point out, enables wealthy districts to support better schools than poor districts can. The court declared the system unconstitutional in California, and efforts are now going forward to repeat this success in other states as well.

• In 1979 New York City parents formed the Education Priorities Panel, inviting civic organizations to join them. Together they confronted the Board of Estimate, forcing the City Council to move $20 million allocated elsewhere into the education budget.

It has become apparent that parents are no longer willing to sit back and let governments and educators decide how to spend their money. As taxpayers, they want to be in ultimate control. They are finally taking that control whenever and wherever they can.

Faculty

As the person closest to a child in his schooling a teacher comes under closest scrutiny by parents. When they do not like what they see, they are beginning to demand change:

• In a rural Midwestern school, parents were dissatisfied over the quality of teachers hired. "The good ones won't come here," the principal offered in explanation, while continuing to staff the school with inexperienced, uncertified faculty. The PTA, refusing to accept his explanation, demanded of the superintendent that the principal be required to hire certified teachers and that at least half the new ones have a minimum of one year's experience. Their demand was met.

• The conservative principal of a New York City school planned to transfer two teachers whom a group of other teachers valued the best in the school. The principal disliked them because they taught in an open class that some parents wanted and that might come to undermine the principal's authority. A group within the PTA, bringing the case to both the Board of Education and the school superintendent, fought to retain the two teachers—and the open classroom—and won.

• A Southern PTA had a teacher fired for "teaching communism" in his Systems of Government course. A group of parents had the dismissal overruled as unconstitutional when they convinced the principal that a course in forms of government could not omit that one form under which almost a third of the world's population lives.

• Although a Western PTA knew it could not fire Mrs. A., a fifth-grade tenured teacher, it forced the principal to give parents a choice of teacher as their children entered fifth grade. When an overwhelming majority steered away from Mrs. A. and could not be convinced to switch in order equalize class size, the principal hired another fifth-grade teacher and transferred Mrs. A. to the administrative staff.

• In upper New York State, a group of parents pulled together in support of a biology teacher to whom the principal wanted to deny tenure because "he taught sex" in his unit on reproduction. "What do you expect him to teach in reproduction?" a parent asked. "Painting?" The teacher got tenure and is still "teaching sex."

Overprotective parents still exist, attacking the teacher for every low grade and for every scolding over misbehavior. They exist in lesser degree, however, because fewer of them are accusing teachers. More are questioning them instead. Knowing this, teachers cannot shrug off parent complaints or demands as interference, as they used to, nor can they pass them on to the principal to be dealt with. They themselves are being held accountable by the parents of children they teach. Their jobs are at stake.

Administration

According to a recent survey, the single factor responsible for quality in a school is the principal. Principals not only *influence* what goes on; they *create* it—through their philosophy of education, their standards, their attitudes toward people, their communicative skills, their flexibility. Therefore, when parents seek administrative changes, they seek to upgrade an institution.

• In a New York City elementary school, a group of parents became increasingly concerned about what they saw as the autocratic and educationally unsound leadership of the principal. Organizing a group of parents within the PTA, they struggled for almost two years with the school, the superintendent, and the Board of Education until at last the principal was unseated.
• In Michigan, parents wanted to include their children in parent-teacher conferences. School policy, issued by the principal, forbade it. Citing Department of Education regulations, parents convinced the principal that in imposing such a restriction, he overstepped his authority. The school now not only allows but advocates three-way teacher-parent-student conferences.
• When the principal of a Northern school refused parents the

right to see their children's files, the PTA reminded him of the Buckley ruling granting them this right by law. They soon saw their children's files.

• In New York City, parents of high school students, displeased with the philosophy and methods of an acting principal, exerted enough pressure on the Board of Education to block a permanent appointment as principal. "They did it with proof, not with screaming," says Nicky Heller, director of the city's United Parents' Association.

• The PTA forced a New England principal, who had initiated a course in sex education, to give them an option of whether or not their children would take it. Although planned as a required course, it is now an elective.

The removal of a top administrator is no easy feat for the PTA, yet with time and persistence it can be done. It *has* been done. Easier and quicker, however, is effecting change in administrative policy. Unseating inevitably leads to hostility over the principal's efforts to secure his or her position and save face. Reversing a policy allows the largesse of "trying a new approach," which includes the PTA as members of a school team.

Curriculum

Curriculum has been the last stand of professionals against the onslaught of parents. "They don't know anything about it," they cry—but parents push on.

• In Missouri, parents were concerned over the lack of career education their children were receiving. They instituted a course and, along with the high school student council, sponsored a Career Day in which community members manned booths. Students, visiting the booths, could get firsthand information on a variety of careers open to them.

• A PTA in California, aghast at the low reading and math scores in their school, created an after-school tutorial program for children, run jointly by them and the school.

• Throughout the state of Florida, PTAs are pressuring local boards to reemphasize basics in all elementary schools.

• In Minneapolis, a reading program was being dropped for lack of funds. Parent pressure, however, grew so strong that, as one of the administrators said, "We had no choice. We had to keep it."

• In Philadelphia, a pilot program of basic skills was tested with three hundred students in one school. When five thousand parents demanded the same for their children, the program was built into the curriculum of sixteen other schools.

• When a group of parents from a central school in the Southwest learned that history was being taught through the inquiry method in a neighboring school, they presented the idea to the faculty committee on curriculum. After a team of parents and teachers visited the other school and reported enthusiastically, the history department reviewed its offerings. By the following year, they revised their curriculum, developing inquiry courses from grades four through nine.

• Some parents, following the example of New York's United Parents' Association, are demanding that schools develop curriculum handbooks for parents. These outline the material to be covered grade by grade, affording parents the opportunity of comparing actual performance with objectives. They are, in effect, making the product accountable for the promise.

Some educators decry parental involvement in curriculum, saying, "You don't tell a carpenter which saw to use." But the simple defense of parents is, "They're our kids, aren't they?" Despite their differences and their fights, parents *are* involved, and educators cannot hold back the tide. What they can do is work *with* parents instead of *against* them. In this way, parents will have a voice in their children's learning, and educators will have a voice in parents' demands.

Governance

The most powerful area in which pressure is making sizable dents is the school's governing body, the Board of Education. Although parents as citizens have always been represented on local boards, their role has tended to be passive. They accepted the status quo, voting on budgets and allocating funds. The position was one of prestige more than of action, and at election time voters knew little and cared less about who ran on the Board of Education slate. As a result, members perpetuated themselves, each other, and an unchallenged viewpoint.

Recently, however, as parents have assumed control of educational aspects *within* their children's school, they have simultaneously assumed control *outside* as well. They have turned the Board of Education into an arm with muscle.

• In a sleepy New York town where a rigidly traditional five-member Board of Education ran a rigidly traditional school, a fight awoke them when a seat on the board was contested by a liberal parent. For weeks phones rang, meetings were held, talk of education echoed where it had never been heard before. The voting turnout was close to 100 percent. The liberal parent won, and the Board of Education has had few sleepy moments since.
• Until a decade ago, New York City schools were under the governance of a central Board of Education. However, while about 50 percent of the student population were minority students, almost 100 percent of the bureaucracy were white middle-class. "How do they know what we want for our children?" parents began to ask. In answer, joined by groups that championed their cause, parents waged a battle for decentralization and community control. Although their proposals were watered down in the resulting bill passed by the state legislature, the establishment of community school boards did give them more of a voice in their children's education.
• Salt Lake City parents have asserted themselves in school decision-making in a system called shared governance. They elect eight members to sit on the School Community Council, which determines educational policy for the district's thirty-seven schools. Their decisions are passed down to a council of educators, which implements them.

Similar steps are being taken by parents throughout the country as both they and professional educators realize the inevitability of their team efforts. Positive results in one community stimulate moves in another as it is seen that joint concerns and endeavors can begin to solve problems and ease tensions. Parents can no longer blame educators for their school problems—they themselves have assumed responsibility for them. Similarly, educators can no longer blame parents for unreasonable demands—they are working shoulder to shoulder with them.

Parents have always had power. Today they are aware of their power and are using it. Where they take it—or where it takes them—depends on their willingness not to dominate but to build themselves inextricably into the school team.

Dear Mrs. Miller:

The mothers in my daughter's class think the teacher is awful. She yells and screams all the time and has the children too afraid to learn. She won't listen to us when we try to talk with her, and we are afraid to go to the principal for fear she will take it out on our children. What can we do?

Mrs. F. L.

Dear Mrs. L.:

Go the PTA president with your problem. PTA members can discuss the situation with the principal without personal involvement and without fear of retaliation. Ask that the principal talk with the teacher— working with her to present other ways of handling children in her class. If she continues as before, the PTA should put pressure on the principal to have her removed . . . or at least give parents the option of transferring their children to another teacher.

Dear Mrs. Miller:

My husband and I and some of our friends feel that the school in our area is really bad. It treats kids like things, not people, and regiments their whole life. We want to start a private, open school where the kids will be happy learning. Where do we begin?

The J.s

Dear Mr. and Mrs. J.:

It won't be easy, but it is possible.

1. Begin by writing to the Commissioner of Education of your state, asking for private school regulations. Write also to the National Association of Independent

Schools, 18 Tremont Street, Boston, Massachusetts, 02108, for any material they have on starting a school.

2. Meet with parents who are or may be interested. Share your findings with them and ask for their feelings and ideas.

3. Appoint committees to gather information. A Finance Committee—to work out budgets. A Fund-raising Committee—to see how and where money can be solicited. A Tuition Committee—to determine how many students the school would need at what cost. A Curriculum Committee—to outline courses in accordance with state requirements.

4. When you meet again with the parents, the findings of these committees will give you an idea of whether or not you have the wherewithal to succeed.

5. If you have, appoint a Board of Trustees and hire an experienced administrator to help you organize.

Good luck!

Dear Mrs. Miller:

Our school is not teaching children metrics, and I think it should. Don't you? Is there any way I can get this subject into the school?

A Worrier

Dear Worrier:

Yes, I think your school should be teaching metrics . . . and I think your state Department of Education would agree. Bring the matter to the attention of the PTA. If they share your concern, let them try to get metrics into the school by working through the principal. That failing, let them try the Superintendent of Schools, the Board of Education, even the State Commissioner if necessary. If the PTA does not espouse your cause, try it alone. One word of warning: don't attack the school for not having initiated the teaching of the metric system. Work with the school, be positive; you have right on your side.

10/Hot Line: Educators to Parents

Dear Teacher,
Today I place my son in your hands for the next important months of his life. I want so much for him that I never had. I do not expect you to spoil him. I want him to learn responsibility. He is often rowdy and difficult to handle, but you are trained in handling kids. You will know what to do. I have found that for a period of his life, you as his teacher will influence him more than I will.

I would like to come to school and talk with you about his progress, but I am afraid it will make you angry. So I will tell you now. You and I are a team. We both want the best for my child. He does his best when we have full cooperation. Please do not hesitate to call me when I need to know something about his behavior. I will believe you if you show you are concerned.

His boisterous attitude is a cover-up for the fact that he is very shy. Please help him to develop a good self-image. Keep track of him, and let him know you are interested in him. You are very good at listening, and you can read between the lines what he is *really* saying to you. Your positive attitude toward learning makes him feel positive about it too. In no way am I holding you totally responsible for his behavior and learning this year. I am a part of your team, and you can be assured that I am backing you at all times.

I want so much for my child—not that he will be rich or famous, but that he can enter the world of work prepared to carry his load. I hope he has learned values, the foundation of a good life—responsibility, honesty, reliability, courage, courtesy—and will have the intelligence to follow through on these values. I want him to feel that in God's scheme for the world, he is important. There is a place for him. But I wish I could protect him from the hard knocks of life. How I wish he could learn from the painful mistakes I have made, but I realize he will have to work through his own life just as I have done in mine.

So, here he is—my son—in your care for a year. Help him respect you, and he will always be grateful that you touched his life.

Sincerely,
Frances Herron

The woman who wrote that letter is a parent. She is speaking for all parents as children begin school, hopeful and new in the fall as crocuses are in the spring.

Scrubbed and clean in their new clothes, children meet their teachers, eyes shining, hearts pounding. This year will be different! As they find their desks, their lockers, their places in line, old fears and failures are forgotten. They greet friends; they size up new classmates. This year will be wonderful! Their teacher is smiling; the paint smells clean; the bell rings loud and clear. They open notebooks. The year lies ahead as unwritten as the first page.

What fills those pages of life in the school year ahead depends on the parents who send their children off and on the teachers with whom they spend each day—on how they share their hopes and support them in the struggles that lie still unmet.

The woman who wrote that letter, Frances Herron, is a teacher as well. She is Oklahoma's Teacher of the Year, selected to represent what is best in teaching as it appears in schools all over the country—perhaps in your school, perhaps in your child's class.

She knows her responsibility to your child. She knows your

responsibility too, for she has been there, where you are. With the same hope and eagerness your child feels, you and she—all parents and teachers—begin school. This year will be different! This year will be wonderful!

My aim in this book has been to help them and you to keep it different, to keep it wonderful, so that the hopes of children will spring anew each day as they enter their classrooms.

Throughout the book, I have discussed your role in your child's education. Let me now share with you some of the wisdom and experience of other educators. The following quotations are compiled from letters and conversations I have had with the country's top educators—Teachers of the Year of every state, National Teachers of the Year, school principals, members of Boards of Education, high-level administrators, college professors.

"What would you like to tell parents," I have asked them, "to help them make school better for their children?"

These are their answers.

On Family

"Children are what they see at home. Be a positive example."

"If there is no unity in your home, your child is lost. Be a family team—discuss, play, work through problems together."

"Be a parent to your son. He doesn't need you as a pal, or as a business success. He needs you to love him and to teach him love and sensitivity."

"With the institution of family becoming shaky all around us, try to make your child strong enough to believe and dare to build a family of his own."

"Remember, the value of time spent with your child is measured in quality, not quantity. If you can't be with your child a lot, then be there totally when you are."

On Discipline

"Don't say, 'I can't do a thing with him' in front of your son. You *can* if you are not afraid to."

"Love your child enough to say, 'No.'"

"Treat your child the way you wish the teacher would."

"Begin teaching your children respect and responsibility when they are little. Then you won't have discipline problems when they are big."

"Let your child accept the consequences of bad behavior. That is the only way to learn how to make decisions."

On Television

"Limit the amount of time children spend in front of the TV set. It is passive entertainment. My students who watch a lot of TV show less imagination and inner resource."

"Don't let young children watch violent TV shows. They cannot cope with them."

"If you watch television with children who are old enough to discuss and question what they see, almost no program can hurt them."

"Don't be afraid to turn off the TV set."

"Whatever you do, don't give your child a private TV set. The best thing about watching is that it brings the family together."

"There are many fine programs on television—Shakespeare, opera, concerts, ballets, political discussions, news. Make sure you and your children watch them."

On Basics

"Basics can be taught through many media, not just workbooks."

"The Back to Basics movement makes parents think any subject but the three R's is pure fluff. Not true. Art, music, physical education, and such are equally important to learning."

"Why all this talk about Back to Basics? Most teachers never left them."

"Don't criticize your teacher for not assigning long dull pages of homework. Drawing a picture may teach your child more."

"Test scores don't reflect basic skills. They just reflect how well children have been drilled to meet the demands of a particular test."

On Facing Problems

"Help your children when they ask for help. Don't force it on them."

"Let your children suffer when they have to. It will teach them that they are strong enough to handle their own problems."

"When your child has a problem at school, don't talk against the teacher or the school. Support them. If you don't, how can you expect the child to learn anything?"

"Children are supposed to have problems. Don't be so horrified—look on them as an opportunity for them to grow."

On Marks

"Encourage your child but don't have unreal expectations. Don't have unreal expectations of me, his teacher, either."

"Rejoice with your child in the positive and help plan and replan for correction of the negative. The person who learns to try is not a failure."

"Don't push for A's. Accept your child at the child's level of development."

"For your child's best effort, say, 'This is good.' Do not say, 'Next time you'll do better.' Maybe the child won't. Or can't."

"Try to find another way to motivate your child to work. Marks aren't given for most of one's life."

On the School-Home Relationship

"Inflation has hit schools as well as pocketbooks. Support your local school budget so that all children can receive adequate education."

"Keep in mind that times have changed and the amount of knowledge is vastly increased. Therefore, schools can't be the way they were when you went to school. What was good for the parents' generation is not necessarily right for today's child."

"The greatest gift we can give our children and ourselves is to be active members of the educational team. It's fun and the best investment of time and energy we make."

"You are your child's first and best teacher. You know more about this person than anyone else."

"Why are you so afraid when your child's teacher tries something new? The old hasn't worked all that well, so why not relax and see what happens?"

"Use your knowledge to help—not fight—your child's teacher.

On Parent-Child Relationships

"Love your children. Give them attention."

"Be a good listener. Show empathy without giving advice. Don't lecture."

"Know your children from the inside out. Don't inflict your interests and viewpoint on them."

"Accept your child as a person of worth, not as an extension of yourself."

"Take time to let your children know you care about them—not only in terms of their progress in school, but in all aspects. If they are sure you care about them, they will care about themselves . . . and then they will do well in school."

So say some of America's leading educators to you, a parent of a child to whom their efforts are directed. They want to make your child's school years the most constructive possible. They need your help.

The years from five to eighteen are precious and short. You leave a little child hesitant at the kindergarten door. Twelve years later an adult emerges, with the wound of separation healed far better than in you.

You have lost a child. You have acquired an adult. The struggle of the metamorphosis has probably left you torn and pained. Where you were sure with the child, now you are uncertain. The question you constantly ponder is, "What did I do wrong?"

Time passes. Your child goes to college or gets a job, marries, and has a family. Your wounds heal over and cover with scar tissue. You accept uncertainty now. You no longer judge. What you did wrong is irrelevant; you stop asking. What you did right begins to show.

You suddenly realize that you like this young person of

yours—not as a child but as an individual. And miracle of miracles this individual likes you. You share interests and laugh together. You express differences, but there is no hostility in them. The common bond of adulthood and parenthood bridges what you used to label the generation gap, and you relate, person to person. You enjoy each other. You accept each other. You are friends.

For me, the peak of parenthood was not holding a newborn infant in my arms, helpless, dependent, satisfying. It is the arms of that infant grown to an adult enfolding me in love. Tests passed or failed, marks high or low, athletic pride or despair are over and done. Gone. What remains is a bond between two people—the person I have grown to be and the person whose growth I have helped shape.

What your child does in school matters less than you think it does at the time. What she or he becomes matters totally. You are a major part of that becoming. You teach your child to love and to give and to lead a life of joy. Therefore, let your hopes and efforts during the school years strive toward these aims, not toward the fleeting ones that loom so large on report cards.

Try to keep your perspective. What matters, matters not for a term or for a year but for a lifetime. A child's most important lessons can be measured only decades after the school bell has ceased to ring.

Keep the long-range view, for as Carlos Castaneda writes in *The Teachings of Don Juan,* "Learning is never what you expect." The focus on your child during the school years should not be on achievement, not on your expectations, but on your child as an individual. You have the power to extend the mere twelve years of school and turn them into a positive lifelong experience.

Do not expect learning to limit itself to skills and scores. Let yourself be surprised at its scope and the depth of its meaning. Then your learning and your child's learning will grow endlessly together, and you will share the miracle.

Index